Zane Grey

Zane Grey

Romancing the West

Stephen J. May

OHIO UNIVERSITY PRESS
ATHENS

Ohio University Press, Athens, Ohio 45701
© 1997 by Stephen J. May
Printed in the United States of America
All rights reserved

Ohio University Press books are printed on acid-free paper ∞ ™
01 00 99 98 97   5 4 3 2 1

Frontispiece: Zane Grey on Don Carlos in the Tonto Basin, Arizona in 1919,
at the zenith of Grey's career. This part of Arizona was one of Grey's favorite
haunts. *Courtesy of the G. M. Farley Collection, Hagerstown, Maryland*

Book design by Chiquita Babb

Library of Congress Cataloging-in-Publication Data

May, Stephen.
　　Zane Grey : romancing the West / by Stephen J. May.
　　　　p.　cm.
　　Includes bibliographical references (p.) and index.
　　ISBN 0-8214-1181-0 (cloth : alk. paper). — ISBN 0-8214-1182-9
　(pbk. : alk. paper)
　　　　1. Grey, Zane, 1872–1939.　2. Novelists, American—20th century—
　Biography.　3. Western stories—History and criticism.　4. West
　(U.S.)—In literature.　I. Title.
　PS3513.R6545Z8　1997
　813' .52—dc21
　　[B]　　　　　　　　　　　　　　　　　　　　　　97-353
　　　　　　　　　　　　　　　　　　　　　　　　　　　　CIP

To the memory of Frank Waters
and Marshall Sprague:
mentors, friends.

"He may be no Henry James, Bret Harte, or Stephen Crane, but in the short run at least, his impact on the American folk mind has been greater than that of those three, or of any other contemporary trio of authors combined. When you think of the West, you think of Zane Grey."

—Frantz and Choate, *The American Cowboy*

Author's Note

Zane Grey changed the spelling of his last name by replacing the *a* with an *e*. To avoid confusion I will use the spelling of *Grey* to refer to Zane Grey only, and the spelling of *Gray* to refer to the rest of the family.

Contents

Illustrations

Preface

In this book about Zane Grey I wished to accomplish several things. Primary among them were: (1) to explore Grey's childhood, especially his relationship with his father; (2) to reveal how this relationship affected his writing, his philosophy, and his emotional life; (3) to show how Grey was predisposed to authoring romances; (4) to discuss Grey's major novels in terms of the parameters of romance; (5) to expose his often ambivalent feelings regarding Mormonism; (6) to trace his development from New York dentist to best-selling Western novelist; (7) to explore the Grey mystique and to place him fairly in twentieth-century literary context. My goal was not to write a full-scale biography, but to focus on the key periods of Grey's life that shaped his major novels. Although he was a perceptive and prolific short story and feature article writer, I have chosen to remain with the novels. Here, I believe, are the windows to Grey's mind. I have first of all endeavored to analyze the man in order to understand his novels, and to explore the novels as a way of understanding the man.

One of the reasons why Grey appealed to me as a literary study was his remarkable staying power in this century. This evidence came to me personally several years ago. While driving through Utah I happened to stop at the house of friend whom I hadn't seen in some time. He lived in a sprawling ranch house deep in the cottonwood and purple sage country that Grey had known so intimately. After he had shown me around the place, we stepped into the living room. In one corner I noticed several bookshelves of Zane Grey books in their familiar beige, blue, and red jackets, which were reprints published by the Walter Black Company. I commented on their good condition. My friend explained that his father had passed the books down to him and that he remained an avid reader of Grey. As he talked, I quickly became aware of the enduring Grey mystique.

When I began writing this book, I often reflected on those shelves of books, in that particular living room, in that rolling sage region, and my friend extolling the qualities of Zane Grey as if he were describing the virtues of a Ming vase or a Rembrandt etching. Those silent shelves of books became a kind of symbolic testament to Grey's persistent legend. This is the legend that I wished to probe in this book. How, after nearly a hundred years of enduring critical scorn, did a popular writer still cling to the public imagination?

One answer seems to be that the land itself chooses the best and worst qualities of its writers and artists. Although it is ultimately undefinable, the American West has a unique place in American letters. For one thing, it is the only region, except perhaps for the South, that comes with the imposing definitives "the" and "American." The American West. What tonnage. Even in our language, we refer to the West as a special place: a place that is not only part of our territory and our history, but part of our imagination as well. It is this place which chose Zane Grey as its spokesman. And for all his defects as a writer, few of his admirers have voiced objections over the years.

Zane Grey appeared in American literature just about the time the frontier era was ending and the vivid memories of it were just beginning to coalesce. Grey never really considered himself simply a writer of westerns, nor was the western his chief influence. Although he kept tabs on other Western writers, he claimed the great European and eastern American authors—Wordsworth, Hugo, Conrad, Hawthorne, and

Cooper—as his literary gods. He was never very comfortable with the mantle of "writer of westerns" until much later in his career, and then he only admitted it only grudgingly.

Variously dubbed the "oater," the "shoot-em-up," or a "blood and thunder" novel, the western emerged during Grey's lifetime as a major literary genre and remains one of the singular American contributions to literature and the cinema. In this study of Grey, I have tried to explain Grey's part in that development. In the tradition of James Fenimore Cooper, Washington Irving, and Owen Wister, Grey championed the role of the frontier in shaping and defining the ideal American character. The great novels of Zane Grey—those discussed in this book—cover the years 1903 to 1926, and are part of the extensive mythology of the West.

Because the phrase "western novel" has traditionally had a pejorative ring to it, Grey and his colleagues have attracted little recent critical attention. One reason clearly is that Grey's brand of romance is out of fashion. In an age that prizes realism and anti-heroism, Grey's distressed women and rescuing knights seem somewhat ludicrous. I have tried to explain in this book that any critical understanding of Grey must include a background in the romance form, for Grey was firstly a writer of romances and secondly a writer of westerns.

Because the writers who influenced Grey make a surprisingly eclectic group, I have endeavored to look both forward and backward in contextualizing his work. There is no question to me that Grey was a 19th nineteenth-century writer trapped in the twentieth century. He fed upon Wordsworth and the romantic poets' worship of nature; he identified with Hawthorne's melancholy, Cooper's individualism, Hugo's social protest, Theodore Roosevelt's vitality, and Wister's knowledge of cowboy lore. Grey was twenty-eight years old when he encountered the twentieth century; however, he felt a distinct obligation to explain the values of the nineteenth century and its great writers. He translated these values and beliefs—morality, heroism, self-sacrifice, honor, chivalry—into stories about the West. In terms of the man himself, however, Grey was not as predictable as his stories. He could be merciless with himself and contemptuous of fellow writers. He hid an enormous amount of shame; his childhood turmoil frequently contributed to periods of depression and immobilization; he had an unappeasable appetite for worldwide adventure, often using it to overcome his blue periods. The late G. M. Farley, a Grey scholar who probably knew him better than anyone else did, once confessed to me that in all of his studies of Grey he always "came up a little short." Perhaps all biographers feel this way. Perhaps all writers defy easy categorization, even though their works are quite accessible. In any event, Grey the man was complex and enigmatic. And I must concur with Farley that, despite all my investigations, the real Zane Grey is an elusive rider escaping into the vast Arizona desert. So it must be.

I have first and foremost striven for historical accuracy. All weather conditions, landscape descriptions, thoughts and feelings recorded here have documentable support. Where it seems called for, the evidence appears in the notes. Any errors of omission or commission are entirely my own.

All quotations from Zane Grey's novels are taken from the reprint editions by Walter J. Black, Inc. (Roslyn, New York).

Finally, I would like to thank some people and agencies that made this book happen. The late Grey scholar G. M. Farley was indispensable in finalizing the manuscript, and I will always remember him as a generous, warm soul; Holly Panich of Ohio University Press provided support and guidance over the years; Senior Editor Gillian Berchowitz and Manuscript Editor Nancy Basmajian of Ohio University Press assisted in making this a much better book. Additionally, I would like to thank the Library of Congress, Washington, D.C.; HarperCollins Publishers, New York; Zane Grey's West Society; Zane Grey, Inc.; and the Colorado Historical Society.

Zane Grey

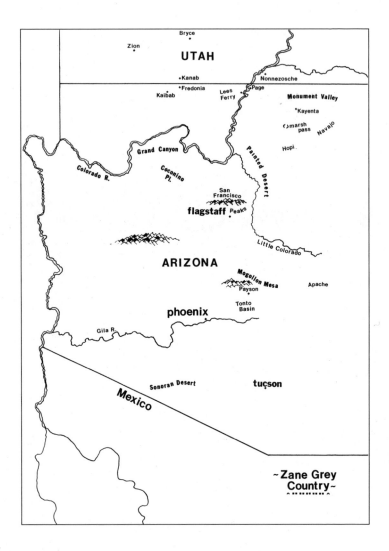

1

Beginnings

Two of the most important people in Zane Grey's early life were complete opposites. The first, his father, Lewis Gray, was fiercely patriarchal, conservative, and nattily attired. His second great influence was named Old Muddy Miser, a gentle, ragged hermit who lived at Dillon's Falls, near Grey's boyhood home of Zanesville, Ohio. Together they helped shape the destiny of young Pearl Zane Grey during his formative years, the 1870s and 1880s in Midwestern America.

Dr. Lewis Gray had coarse, sallow skin, penetrating blue eyes, a walrus mustache, a little cleft chin, and an air of aristocracy. He was a traditionalist in just about everything. He believed that children should be seen and rarely heard. The cane was close at hand, and he would use it liberally, justifying his violence against his children by maintaining that it was for their own good. From a very early age, Zane Grey knew this sudden violence could occur, and he feared provoking his father.

Dr. Gray wanted Zane to grow up to be like him—a dentist. Every action, nearly every conversation between father and son seemed to anticipate this end. Young Zane would be a dentist, whether he wanted to be or not. His father was not above resorting to emotional manipulation of the young boy. As it happened, a suitable opportunity for an object lesson was close at hand: a trail they traveled from Zanesville to Dillon's Falls snaked past the poorhouse. On one occasion they stopped and Dr. Gray pulled the dark-haired Zane to his side, pointing to the poorhouse with his crooked walking stick. "If you don't learn to like work and study," said Dr. Gray, "that's where you'll wind up, like Old Muddy Miser."[1]

Dr. Gray continued to fear the corrupting influence of Old Miser and warned Zane to keep away from him. But Zane didn't. He began a relationship with the fisherman that lasted several years. At a later time, Grey's mother admonished him: "A fisherman is a lazy bad boy grown up. . . . He always carries a bottle. You've seen drunken men. Well, that's what fishing and a bottle does."[2]

And so Zane was raised in a household where engaging in juvenile and impractical pursuits—fishing, pleasure reading, and writing—was discouraged and criticized. Because of this, Grey created a secret world in his teens, known only to him, his brother, and his friends. At the heart of this hidden world was Old Muddy Miser, the haggard, gap-toothed hermit who became a mediator between the stifling world of Zane's restrictive parents and the wild, imaginative truant life. By becoming a kind of woodland crone to young Grey, Old Muddy helped ease him into adulthood by lessening his fears about fishing and other "foolish" activities. At home in Zanesville Grey was met with suspicion and distance; but at Dillon's Falls he communed with his shaggy mentor, learning woodlore and various fishing techniques.

Years later, Grey would remember Old Muddy's exact words to him:

"I've read a good deal about salmon and trout; and you, no doubt, will go far afield from Dillon's Falls and catch these fish. I have also read a great deal about the big saltwater fish of the Seven Seas. Nobody seems to have caught these strange, fierce fish of the salty seas, and I wonder why this is so. Surely someday somebody will venture to go after these giant fish. Perhaps you will be the one. I wish I could live to have you tell me about them. You must make fishing a labor of love, no matter what your vocation might be. You must make time for your fishing. . . . And here is the most cardinal and important point. Don't drink. For some strange reason, most fishermen drink, and many of them are drunkards. Some men fish solely to earn money to buy liquor. Others seem to go fishing to find a time and a place to drink. Whiskey is an abomination for anyone, and especially a fisherman."[3]

Of course Grey would go on to become a great fisherman, omnivorous reader, successful author, superlative truant—and stern teetotaler—and he could trace it all back to several forest sojourns with a gray-haired gnome called Old Muddy Miser.

The Zane family tradition was firmly rooted in the culture of midwest America. The family, however, had its origins in Denmark. An early Zane migrated to England in the sixteenth century and from him descended Robert Zane, a clothmaker, who in turn immigrated to the American colonies, settling in New Jersey. Eventually a family member moved to Virginia. After the middle of the eighteenth century Ebenezer Zane, a grandson of the Virginia Zane, headed over the Appalachians from Virginia and settled in the forests of the Ohio River Valley. Accompanying him on this journey were his three brothers and their friends the McCullochs and the Wetzels. They selected a spot on an island along the east bank of the Ohio River and built a crude settlement, the site of today's Wheeling, West Virginia. Ebenezer Zane soon returned to Virginia, gathering his family and preparing to make the island his fortress and home.

Later a stockade was built and christened Fort Henry. When the Revolutionary War broke out, Ebenezer Zane was commissioned a colonel of the Virginia militia and placed in charge of the fort. On three occasions the British and the Indians unleashed violent attacks on the fort. It was during one of these assaults in 1782 that the colonel's young sister, Betty Zane, rose to heroic stature by carrying gunpowder in her apron through a storm of gunfire and smoke. Everyone in Zanesville knew of the exploits of Betty Zane and of her remarkable journey from the arsenal to the fort. Grandfathers used to tell the stories over the fire while young 'uns like Zane Grey listened spellbound, moved by the idea that someone of such apparent innocence could accomplish a task so daring and arduous. And, too, she was kinfolk!

After the conflict at Fort Henry, Colonel Ebenezer Zane, Pearl Zane Grey's great-grandfather, went on to greater fame. In 1796, President George Washington selected Zane, now the proprietor of a trading post on the Ohio River, to open a road from Fort Henry to present-day Maysville, Kentucky. Zane and his brother Jonathan helped blaze the trail through the wilderness. Zane's Trace, as the road became known, opened the western territories to eastern pioneers. As a reward for the Colonel's services, Congress granted him several military warrants upon sections of land, each a square mile in size. From these warrants came the villages and later the cities of Martin's Ferry, Bridgeport, and Zanesville, Ohio.

Until his death in 1812, Ebenezer Zane kept a diary—or so Zane Grey claimed, although it has not survived—chronicling his daily routines as well as the bitter and exciting years at Fort Henry. After the Colonel's death, the diary was passed down to family members, until it fell into the hands of Zane Grey in the 1880s. Grey maintained the fragile diary into his thirties, purportedly using it to relate the historical events in his first novel, *Betty Zane*.

After the passing of Colonel Zane, the city of Zanesville flourished. Located about seventy-five miles due west of old Fort Henry, the town served as state capital of Ohio from 1810 to 1812. Colonel Zane's descendants were part of Zanesville's rapid growth in the 1820s and 1830s, when the city's pottery factories gained recognition.

Zane's father, Lewis M. Gray, enters the picture around the middle of the nineteenth century, when, after a failed attempt to enter the ministry, he came to Zanesville, courted and eventually married a woman named Josephine Zane, and hung out his shingle as a doctor of dentistry. From their marriage came five children: Lewis Ellsworth, Ella, Ida, Pearl Zane (born January 31, 1872), and Romer Carl (born 1875).

The name Pearl is thought to have originated with Queen Victoria's love of clothes colored pearl gray, although Zane also had a male cousin named Pearl. Since Zane's parents admired the reigning queen, they thought the name Pearl was both suitable and a token of their admiration. The saddling of Grey with a feminine name, however, gives some indication of his parents' insensitivity to *his* welfare. He was to bear the burden of his first name for close to thirty years before his career as a writer began in earnest, and then he dropped it like a piece of cumbersome and unwanted baggage.

꙳

Zane Grey's boyhood was both idyllic and painful. He grew up in a modest house at 363 Convers Avenue in Zanesville. The city boasted about 9,500 residents, a population stabilized by the town's position in the rural heartland of southeastern Ohio. Rolling meadows surrounded the house and stretched to the nearby Muskingum River, whose waters were rich in catfish and mysterious enough to lure the schoolboys from their homes and studies.

In October, Zane and his brothers and sisters would rake the leaves into piles, and their father would come by and set fire to them. Soon the air was redolent with the smell of burning leaves, and great balloons of smoke eddied over the patches of forest until the wind collapsed and scattered them.[4]

Zane stuck close to younger brother Romer during his early youth. Arm in arm, their poles balanced jauntily over their shoulders, they whistled down the lanes leading to the river. Or, if they were goaded by some rowdy boys, they took them on no matter how greatly they were outnumbered. Zane frequently fought boys larger than he, particularly when Romer was threatened. Grey always had a quick temper, especially in his teens, and almost any taunt could easily provoke him.[5]

On Sunday afternoons in summer, when Zane wasn't fishing or

reading, he stood over his father on the huge balustraded veranda, fanning him in the July heat. These situations always evoked ambivalent feelings in Zane. On the one hand he wished to be close to his father and defuse any anger he might be feeling that day. On the other hand he desperately wanted to be fishing with the other boys. When Dr. Gray's eyelids drooped and he began snoring, Zane tiptoed from the veranda, grabbed his pole, and dashed to the fishing hole.[6]

Or in winter, Lewis Gray, who liked to eat fresh snow, would demand that young Zane bring him pails of new-fallen snow. So Zane was sent out again and again to satisfy his father's appetite.

Despite this callous treatment (and in some cases because of it), Zane bonded to his father much more than he did to his mother. Dr. Gray prided himself on his firm control of his children and ran his household with Prussian rigidity. The images of a son fanning his father or scooping up pails of snow, of a boy silently pleading for some affection, only accentuate the idea that Dr. Gray's main concern was to be revered as a stern and unapproachable patriarch.

Sealed off from any nurturing relationship with his parents, Grey retreated into reading, particularly during the long insular winters when the snowbanks hugged the windowsills and Zanesville napped silently in its arctic tomb. He devoured *Robinson Crusoe*, James Fenimore Cooper's Leatherstocking Tales, and the popular Harry Castlemon books. Cooper particularly fired his imagination, providing him a dangerous and sinister historical landscape beyond the confines of Ohio. In addition to Cooper's exciting narrative, Grey was also intrigued by the illustrations, in this case by Felix Darley. Even at fifteen Zane was a fairly good artist, and he spent many hours honing his drawing ability. He grew up at a time when noted artists like Darley, Howard Pyle, Frederic Remington, Henry Farny, and Edwin Abbey were guiding America into her golden age of illustration (1880–1900). He pored over the drawings with as much enthusiasm as he followed the storyline. Like other authors (Hemingway among them) Grey early on sharpened his descriptive skills by analyzing the work of talented visual artists.

After Fenimore Cooper, the work that influenced Grey the most was Charles McKnight's *Our Western Border* (1876). Describing the exploits of the early settlers of the Ohio River Valley, *Our Western Border* provided Grey endless hours of absorbing reading and he returned to its pages continuously through his teens and into his adulthood.

It was during this crucial period, between the ages of twelve and fifteen, that Zane Grey decided to become a writer. He did not mention this decision to his mother and father. He didn't dare. He outwardly acknowledged that he would pursue a career in dentistry, but inwardly he committed himself to a life in literature.

He wrote his first story at the age of fifteen, a grotesquely juvenile work called "Jim of the Cave." However, it was not its literary content but the incidents surrounding its creation that constituted the significant aspect of his writing debut. Zane had written the story in a secluded cave behind the Gray home. Outfitted with kitchen utensils pirated from the house, and festooned with feathers, animal skins, and primitive odds and ends, the cave was the perfect place for Zane and his friends to read, write, eat candy, and swap tall stories.

Eventually Dr. Gray discovered the location of the cave and clambered down the ledge to investigate. No one was around. Inside he recognized several utensils that had mysteriously vanished over the preceding months. He also discovered Zane Grey's handwritten story. He was thumbing through it when Zane stumbled in. Enraged to think that his son was wasting time at such a foolish endeavor, he tore up the manuscript in front of Zane, punishing him with a vigorous tongue-lashing. He then proceeded to thrash his son with a strip of carpet, to heap scorn on writing as sheer nonsense, and to reiterate that it was time for Zane to resume his dentistry studies. Dazed, angered, and ashamed, Zane left the cave and resigned himself to an endless routine of washing windows and brushing plaster of paris from tarnished sets of teeth.

It is difficult to calculate the degree of humiliation and rage felt by Grey. Doubtless it was sharp and profound. The great authority figure in his life, his father, had passed judgment on his chosen career, and the incident reinforced the notion that writing was indeed "foolish" and dentistry practical and respectable. Certainly the event in the cave was disturbing and far-reaching because it tended to repeat itself every time Grey tried to write and was rejected. Every rebuff and criticism only magnified the idea that his writing was no good, and hence, that he was no good. And so his career in literature became not only a humiliating exercise in self-doubt, but also a tortuous, exhausting attempt to earn a living in which he was haunted by his father's scorn.

In 1890, three years after the cave incident, Dr. Lewis Gray returned home from Washington, D.C. and bitterly announced that he had squandered the family fortune in a bad investment. Ashamed to continue business in Zanesville, he moved his family to Columbus, Ohio.[7] Zane was eighteen and able to get a job as an usher in a theater, while brother Romer drove a delivery wagon. Dr. Gray never recovered emotionally or physically from his financial ruin. Zane assumed more and more of his father's dentistry duties, on one occasion traveling into a nearby village to pull teeth from a dozen patients who had assembled at a hotel.

Zane became swept up in the activities in Columbus, a city five times the size of Zanesville. It offered numerous exciting diversions for a young man. The town boasted several good baseball teams, and Zane quickly became a pitcher for the Capitals. A scout for the University of Pennsylvania spotted his pitching talents one day and offered him a scholarship if he proved himself as a player. He declined similar offers from Vanderbilt and Chicago Wesleyan, opting to play for Penn because of its highly touted dentistry program.

With the pressures of combining baseball and academics, Grey slowly pushed his writing aside. He loved playing baseball, but had to endure an erratic academic four years marked by scholastic indifference, loneliness, and sophomoric brawling.

A Pearl on the Diamond

Baseball—not literature, and certainly not chemistry or biology—ruled Grey's life at the University of Pennsylvania during the years 1892–1896.

Since the first intercollegiate game in 1859, when Amherst whipped Williams College 73–32, baseball had increasingly gained prominence in college athletic programs. On the professional level, a National League was formed in 1876. By 1882 the American Baseball Association was organized, and the sport entered the era of big business. During the 1880s the first crop of baseball stars emerged. Among them were players like King Kelly, Charles Comiskey, Roger Conner, and Pete Browning. They were true nonconformists and hell-raisers. Kelly, for example, when asked if he drank during the game, replied, "It depends on the length of the game." At first base, Comiskey bombarded opposing batters and runners with endless profanities. Conner became the Babe Ruth of early baseball, swatting 136 home runs in his brief career. And Browning, known as the gladiator of the Louisville Eclipse,

Grey *(second from right, second row)* and the University of Pennsylvania baseball team, c. 1895. He remained a baseball fan throughout his life, writing articles and short stories about the sport, playing on amateur teams, and attending professional games. *Courtesy of the G. M. Farley Collection, Hagerstown, Maryland*

pioneered the use of the Louisville Slugger bat. At one time Browning had two hundred of them—all named after people in the Bible. These, and other players, helped make the game into what Mark Twain called, "the very symbol, the outward expression of the drive and push and rush and struggle of the raging, tearing, booming, 19th century."

When Pearl Zane Grey arrived in Philadelphia to attend college, he settled in some cheap rooms on Market Street. He soon headed to the ballpark where the team was preparing for a game against Riverton. Grey was promised a scholarship if he proved himself on the field. Like most untested freshmen, however, he was quickly shunned during practice. Varsity players like Coogan, Boswell, and the captain, Hollister, kept to themselves.

The director of athletics, a man named Madeira, thought Grey was ready to pitch against Riverton. Coogan, however, declared that Pearl Zane was too much a greenhorn to risk against the Riverton bats. Madeira listened to his players but made no decision.

When the University of Pennsylvania Quakers played Riverton that Saturday, Madeira started Boswell on the mound. By the fifth inning, the Quakers trailed Riverton 4–2. Boswell was clearly out of steam. Madeira thought of trying the young Ohioan, Pearl Zane Grey. The varsity players, on the other hand, voiced their disapproval. Grey went out to pitch the top of the sixth. One batter popped up in the infield; the second clubbed a grounder; the third struck out. Grey brimmed with sudden confidence. He had a good rhythm going, marked by a good fastball, a change-up, and his best pitch, a wicked curveball.

In the bottom of the inning, Penn tied the score. Grey returned to the mound and blanked Riverton through eight innings. By the tenth inning, with the score knotted at 4–4, a Penn man led off with a base hit. Grey came to the plate and hit a double in the gap in center. The Quakers won, and Grey was something of a hero. The Riverton game, a minor rite of passage for Grey, meant a tuition scholarship for him. However, he still had to come up with money for lab equipment, books, and lodging. He took a job in the college restaurant, but he hated it. He simply was too embarrassed to wait on his fellow players. Later, he ushered at football games, but even this menial labor bothered him.[1]

In the middle of his first year at Penn, Grey developed a fairly predictable routine: playing baseball, shooting pool at a west Philadelphia poolroom, holing up at the university library, and studying—sparingly it turned out—for his dentistry courses. Mechanical and operative dentistry proved to be a rugged program. He loathed physiology and anatomy. Chemistry, taught by Professor Wormly, turned out to be one of his stiffest courses. He increasingly liked his histology class, taught by Robert "Bobby" Formad. But baseball and writing romantic poetry in the library became alternatives to studying, and he gradually pushed his textbooks aside.

At the library he read Kipling and Stevenson, and wrote some poems in the manner of Tennyson, Swinburne, and Wordsworth.[2] The romantic in Grey was beginning to emerge. He later wrote that his "thoughts wandered afar, if not in green fields and quiet woods, then to dreams of what might come true. In truth, I was a poor student." He dreamed of becoming a writer, but the practical side of Grey reminded him that he should probably go into a respectable profession like dentistry. Besides, his family was backing him in such an endeavor. Even though Grey resigned himself to the program, he buried his anguish in sports and reading.

If Grey's personal reading of novels tended to be decidedly romantic and escapist, his academic reading for literature and history covered the American and European classics. College professors of the 1890s, especially those teaching arts and history, felt the pull of two divergent trends. On one hand they felt compelled to worship the wealth of European masterworks in art and literature, and to show students their influence on American culture. On the other, teachers struggled to include works in the curriculum which reflected truly American themes. After the Civil War, in an era that became known as the "Gilded Age," a growing artistic connection to Europe gathered strength. Of American novelists, Henry James embodied this aggressive European sensibility. Even by the 1890s, the twenty-one-year-old Zane Grey was lectured on the merits of Dickens, Thackeray, Hugo, Flaubert, and Balzac. He, of course, loved their stories, but their settings alienated him. Like Cooper and Hawthorne, he was conservative to the core. Early on, and later throughout his life, he adopted and promoted a vigorously American outlook.

In the 1880s this distinctly American literature began to assert itself. Discovering that America had a unique present and "a useable past" (in the words of Van Wyck Brooks), William Dean Howells and Sarah Orne Jewett espoused a version of American realism in fiction. Howells, in particular, found his way into the classroom. But the distinct Yankee voice was Mark Twain, who in *Huckleberry Finn* (1884) started a whole trend in modern American literature. At the heart of this movement was the belief in the frontier.

Twain and later writers promoted the notion that the American frontier symbolized mobility and purity. However, by the time that Grey was matriculating at the University of Pennsylvania, the era of the American frontier, for all practical purposes, was over. As a myth, though, the frontier endured in the popular mind and in fiction into the next century, with Zane Grey becoming one of its chief exponents.

The American wilderness was also a myth about space, where men and women measured their freedom and independence by the distance from one another. As urban crowding and slums threatened post-Civil War America, writers and observers found comfort in the early golden days of frontier and provincialism. Henry Adams, for example, in his *History of the United States of America during the Administration of Thomas Jefferson* (1889), promoted this anti-modern viewpoint. Adams despaired at the plight of late-nineteenth-century America with its excess, corruption, and urbanism. Yearning for the order and beauty of the Jeffersonian age, he lashed out at industrialism and the lack of values in contemporary culture. Zane Grey, a chronic Huck Finn, absorbed a significant amount of this reflective thinking as a student.

Also coursing through nineteenth-century American thought was the idea that the frontier invited a certain anarchy. In *The Oregon Trail* (1849) Francis Parkman speaks of his journey west as a passage "out of bounds," as if the moral and spatial restrictions of the east had no credence west of the Mississippi. And perhaps they didn't. But central to the myth of the frontier is the belief that they didn't, combined with a desire to make it a fraternity—backward certainly—but free.

How could people live happy and productive lives in anarchy? Later, this became one of the central dilemmas facing Grey's fiction. Grey succumbed to the current thinking on Social Darwinism mixed with a strong secular Calvinism. He would later create a "code" of the frontier for his characters. If the elect few accepted this code, they would prosper and receive enlightenment; however, the majority were damned because they refused to adopt this code and struggled in darkness.

Grey came to view the frontier, particularly that of the Southwest, as the antidote to the moral corruption of his day. Pearl Zane Grey was only twenty-two when Frederick Jackson Turner delivered his famous speech, "The Significance of the Frontier in American History" in 1893, but Grey went on developing, and frequently over-developing, Turner's ideas throughout his long career as a novelist.

Meanwhile, Zane Grey drifted into the life of a loner. Swearing off alcohol further removed him from the male bonding rituals of parties and game celebrations. He rarely wrote to his mother and father in Ohio. His beloved brother R.C. was playing semi-professional baseball in Delphos, Ohio. Outside of baseball, Grey did not develop a significant relationship, especially with a woman, while at the university.

When February 15 came each year and baseball practice started, Grey went to the mound and worked on his curveball. But changes loomed on the horizon that threatened to shatter his chances for a career in baseball.

Ironically, it was a fellow Ohioan who helped seal Grey's fate. His name was Denton True "Cy" Young. Known as "the Phenom" when he first played for the Cleveland Spiders in August of 1890, Young quickly humiliated batters with his arsenal of pitches. Young went on to become one of the immortals of the game. Another pitcher, Amos Rusie of the New York Giants, was nearly the equal of Young. Rusie's fastball was so powerful that it forced his catcher to load his mitt with lead to soften the impact. Because of the power of these and other pitchers, the National League in 1893 voted to move the pitching mound back to the present distance of sixty feet six inches. Colleges quickly complied with the new rule, including the University of Pennsylvania.

Grey tried to make his curveball work from the new distance, but to

GREY WAS THE HERO

He Made a Home Run, Triple and Several Singles and Was Responsible for Several Runs—— Quakers Played Poorly.

Newspaper clipping from the 1890s showing Grey in his favorite role of sports hero. Although he did poorly in his college courses, he proved to be a scrappy, versatile baseball player. *Courtesy of the G. M. Farley Collection, Hagerstown, Maryland*

no avail. He lost his magic, his confidence, and in turn, his position on the mound. For Grey, who craved being the hero, it was an enormous setback. Grey, however, could still hit, and he was moved to the outfield. Meanwhile the university passed a rule that mandated a player would have to pass an exam in each course in order to remain on the team. Grey was grossly unprepared. He barely passed his exam in therapeutics. Professor Wormly, realizing that Grey spent more time playing baseball than studying chemistry, gave his student the lowest possible passing grade. In the histology lab Dr. Bobby Formad gave him a 99 out of a possible 100—due in large part to Pearl Zane's drawing ability. Formad's high grade boosted Grey's overall average and salvaged his remaining academic and sporting years.

Toward the end of his years at Penn, Grey and the Quakers beat the New York Giants in an exhibition game. That year they also bested Johns Hopkins, Lehigh, Harvard, and Cornell. Playing in the outfield now, Grey tried to play the role of the clutch hitter to impress his team and fans.

In the last game of his college days, Penn played the University of Virginia. The Quakers struggled through the game, making inept plays and swinging wildly at the plate. Penn batted in the bottom of the ninth, trailing Virginia. With two men out and a runner on second, Grey approached the plate.[3] Borrowing a page from the popular writer Horatio Alger, Grey promptly swatted a home run and won the game for the Quakers. He was the campus hero.

Metaphorically, Grey's minute at the plate is significant. He continued trying to renew that triumphant moment throughout his life, and more importantly, to recreate it in his fiction.

New York

Leaving Philadelphia after graduation, Grey arrived in New York City in 1896. He was twenty-four and apparently resigned to making a living as a dentist in a town already thronged with established and eager young doctors. But he calculated, too, that he was close to the beat of literary life and perhaps that nearness could ignite fresh life in his writing.

His appearance had changed little since he had scrapped and fished in Zanesville. He was a shade under five feet nine inches tall with a tough, wiry frame. His dark hair parted in the middle; he had an Anthony Perkins–like intensity, searching dark eyes, and a jaw thrust resolutely forward. In numerous photographs he does not smile. Frequently he glances away from the viewer as if in shame, or as if he wishes to be somewhere else. Indeed, it is the expression of someone not wishing to be known.

During this settling-in period, Zane changed the spelling of his name from Gray to Grey. The reason for this unusual change remains speculative. Was he using the British spelling merely as an affectation, or was he subtly but deliberately endeavoring to separate himself from his family name?[1]

Whatever the reason, Grey hung out his shingle at 100 West 74th St. bearing the name "Dr. P. Zane Grey." Pulling teeth helped keep his pitching arm in shape, and on weekends he fled New York for Orange, New Jersey, where he played for the local team. He was also a strong hitter and enjoyed swatting clutch hits to help his team win in the closing innings. Often, however, the word got out that he was a dentist, prompting some of the players to ask him about dental problems between innings.

For the first four years in New York, dentistry was pure toil and frustration. It is possible, nonetheless, to discern a link between it and his other career that was slowly to emerge. Even at the turn of the century, tooth extraction was still violent and painful surgery. Through performing countless extractions, Grey had become desensitized to this violence in the dentist's chair and that desensitization becomes apparent in his early writing and sporadically throughout the later novels. In a particularly gory example from his second novel, *The Spirit of the Border* (1906), the scout Lew Wetzel drives a "quivering dripping blade" into the groin of a foe, "through flesh and bone hard and fast."[2] The victim dies a repulsive, lingering death while buzzards tear at his flesh. The modern reader might find such gruesome details commonplace, but the early-twentieth-century reader, unaccustomed to pervasive violence, found them shocking and disturbing. In his brief introduction to the book, Grey admitted that there was "brutality" in the novel but that it "was true to the life of the Western border." Despite this claim of authenticity, Grey felt impelled to tone down the violence in later novels. Perhaps he felt guilty—guilty at his unabashed approach to the grotesqueries he had witnessed firsthand in surgery. But he eventually realized he could not relate this violence to his readers and still remain a popular writer.

Between the years 1896 and 1900, Grey did his best to burrow into New York culture, to the extent a corn-fed, midwestern outdoorsman could. He continued to play baseball and to show up at his dental office. He attended both comic and dramatic theater presentations and dreamed of his own ascendance as a writer. He was not seeing a particular woman on a steady basis, and since it was difficult for him to make friends, bouts of loneliness and immobilization were common.

During the winter months when the city was spellbound in darkness and chill, Grey returned early to his cramped quarters, read, and resurrected the idea of becoming a writer. He turned for inspiration to such writers as Hugo, Kipling, and Robert Louis Stevenson. Stevenson, especially, was the literary idol of Grey's generation. Both Stevenson and Grey were masters of romance writing. Of course Stevenson's venues included the Scottish highlands and the lush tropics, but Grey's interest in him went beyond locales. The central features of the romance—distinct good and evil forces, the heroic journey, the mistaken identity, etc.—were universal and Grey could easily transport them to the deserts and mesas of the American West. Additionally, Darwin's and Spencer's ideas on natural selection impressed him deeply and he began adopting them as part of his own personal philosophy. They were to show up in various guises in numerous Grey novels.[3] Studying other writers' styles, he tried to work on his own and felt the early pain of inadequacy and the slow knife of self-rejection. He sweated over his blossoming prose style, secretly cursing himself for not studying grammar and syntax instead of fishing and playing baseball. It was typical for Grey to be merciless on himself, and this treatment would translate into serious emotional problems as the years progressed.

Through four cheerless New York winters, he studied, analyzed, practiced, and worshipped at the feet of all literary gods he hoped to emulate.

During this period his brother Romer (called R.C.), also a reluctant dentist now, migrated to New York City. They immediately began hanging around together, renewing the closeness they had felt in Zanesville. One day in August 1900 they packed up their fishing gear and headed west to one of their favorite spots on the Delaware River, Zane toting a Brownie camera for the occasion. They were near Lackawaxen, Pennsylvania, soon to become Grey's home. Paddling close to the New Jersey shore, they encountered a party of young women picnicking under the trees. Among them was Lina Elise Roth, age seventeen, who proceeded to carry on a lengthy flirtation with Zane as he rested in the boat. Zane and R.C. later beached the canoe and joined the women on the shore.

Lina Roth, called Dolly by her friends, was a student at the Normal School of the City of New York and intended to complete her studies at Columbia University to become a teacher. She was a voracious reader and student of literature, two virtues which would have important consequences in her relationship with Grey. Of German heritage, Dolly was plump of figure with a broad, Teutonic face and a beaming expression. She had an engaging smile and an infectious warmth that attracted Grey.

They continued dating throughout the autumn of 1900 and into the winter months of 1901. Most of the time Grey visited Dolly at her mother's home, which was near Grey's dental office on West 74th Street. Or later they met at the many tea shops in Manhattan. They were soon swept away and entered that rapturous state of mind that the British writer H. E. Bates called "a sacred, suspended, breathless, often wordless, vacuum."[4]

Grey poured out his heart to Dolly in his letters, and she responded with passionate, swooning, often tearful, seven- and eight-page epistles of her own. Grey frequently lashed out at Dolly, blaming her for inconsequential things that nettled him at the moment. He would realize his error and end up apologizing, sometimes for two to three days after the incident.

Grey continued to be afflicted with bouts of depression, in which his rage, so long shoved down, began to overwhelm him. These bouts would persist all his life, interrupting his writing routine and destroying his most restful and contemplative leisure moods. Doubtless this anger had been simmering for a long time inside him. He had stored up

R.C. Grey *(left)* and Zane Grey on a fishing adventure, c. 1900–1901, around Grey's thirtieth birthday. The brothers remained close even after Zane moved to California. *Courtesy of the G. M. Farley Collection, Hagerstown, Maryland*

a heap of rejection and shame and every fresh rebuff, however innocent, only made it swell and multiply. Unable to vent his frustration in a healthy fashion, he turned it on himself and ultimately fell victim to it.

Whole weeks passed in which these black moods shrouded his mind and thoughts. Writing often did not help because it raised the angry voice of a father who had reprimanded him for the very act. Fishing helped, but one couldn't fish one's entire life. The bouts had to be endured. In his defiance he could sound like Lord Byron: "A hyena lying in ambush—that is my black spell!—I conquered one mood only to fall prey to the next. And there have been days of hell. Hopeless, black, morbid, sickening, exaggerated mental disorder. I know my peril—that I must rise out of it, very soon for good and all, or surrender forever. It took a day—a whole endless horrible day of crouching in a chair, hating self and all, the sunshine, the sound of laughter, and then I wandered about like a lost soul or a man who was conscious of imminent death . . ."[5] Grey plodded through the days with no help, hoping for some pinprick of light to shine however dimly in the darkness. As time passed, the grim, unsmiling man in the photographs began to withdraw from a threatening world.

Fishing and playing baseball—later hunting and wandering—were escapes from intolerable reality. Grey remarked that he could not "stand the truth. Realism is death to me. I cannot stand life as it is."[6] Writing was also a seductive diversion, but it had its price. On one hand it was a pleasurable escape from the rigors of life. That was the part that attracted Grey. But on the other hand, it presented its own set of demands, frustrations, schedules, rules, and veiled demons which brought him face to face with the reality he sought desperately to avoid. He wrote that there was "always an extreme difficulty in the taking up again of the habit of writing. . . . I am tortured before I can begin to write. This morning I had no desire to write, no call, no inspiration, no confidence, no joy. I had to for myself."[7]

In many ways Zane Grey simply refused to grow up and accept the responsibilities of adulthood. Because of this refusal he resorted to the activities that he had loved as a boy. At twenty-eight, forty-four, or sixty years of age, he was trapped in the enthusiasms of a fifteen-year-old. He wrote from this ego state, producing the romantic narratives and superheroes of a world far better, and certainly more comfortable, than any real one. This perhaps explains why Grey's work never matured beyond the formulaic western romance and why his novels tend to be youth-induced searchings for an idealized and ordered world.

~🐎~

While Dolly attended college, Grey went through the motions at his office and returned in the early evening to write under an oil lamp which feebly lit his shabby tenement. His dentistry career continued to frustrate him, and there is no doubt that by 1902, and his thirtieth birthday, he deeply resented his prescribed vocation. He increasingly turned to writing to offset his sense of futility. In May 1902 his first article "A Day on the Delaware" was published in *Recreation*. Later, in February 1903, *Field and Stream* bought "Camping Out," and it was published under the byline "P. Zane Grey." Both articles reflected his fishing and outdoors knowledge, and their success tempted him to do more. He returned to his kitchen table and the faint glow of the oil lamp, easing himself into the role of the stereotypical fledgling author who writes his heart out in one of the dusky corners of Gotham and hungers for more fortune.

By the summer of 1902 he had decided to write a novel. Articles were modestly lucrative, but he knew the truly great writers proved themselves with a novel. He wanted to join the ranks of emerging writers: Jack London, Frank Norris, Upton Sinclair, Booth Tarkington, and a young upstart named Owen Wister, who had just written a magnificent book of the West, *The Virginian*. Grey systematically digested Wister's novel, studying how its author blended narrative, dialogue, and description. Grey loved *The Virginian* and wanted to write a book similar to it. But he had not been west. He had experienced the American West only through countless pulp novels, illustrations, and photographs.

What he *did* know was the story of the Zanes and their struggles in the Ohio River Valley during the Revolutionary War. He decided to retell the story of Betty Zane by fleshing out character, embellishing plot, and providing a convincing historical atmosphere for the action. James Fenimore Cooper would again be his literary guide, and from him and all the other adventure writers who followed Cooper, Grey could inherit a tradition and offer his own unique contribution to it.

Heir to the Tradition

It is not too much to say that nearly the entire American romance tradition, in which Grey was to play a major role, rests on the slender shoulders and acute sensibilities of one gifted writer: James Fenimore Cooper.

Cooper began his career with dramatic flourish. After becoming dissatisfied with an English novel he had been reading, he angrily threw it aside and announced to his family that he could write a better one. And so he set out to do just that. In 1821 his first novel, *Precaution,* appeared. Cooper followed his mildly successful first effort with *The Spy* (1821). After the huge success of *The Last of the Mohicans* (1826), Cooper wrote *The Prairie* in 1827, the first book of the Leatherstocking Tales to have a setting in the American West. *The Prairie* is set in Iowa, and considering that Cooper had never been west, the rolling, featureless plains seemed a safe venue for his story. The novel recounts the adventures of Natty Bumppo, the granite-boned frontiersman, who untangles evil and goes directly to the heart of the problem. This directness appealed deeply to young Zane Grey, who created characters in the Natty mold. Grey, like Natty, saw that a strong, noble character could accomplish things that an inept and often corrupt legal system could not.

One of the major defects of *The Prairie* is that it simply lacks the necessary verisimilitude to make it believable. Since Cooper had not been west, he relied on some of the reports of the time to make his setting convincing. One of his goals was to extend the limits of the known frontier and reveal how the westward movement was affecting America's vision. The novel is full of descriptions of characters and Indian encampments, but rarely does Cooper describe the intervals of landscape: creeks flowing, hawks soaring, and rabbits scurrying. Cooper's naive and romantic view of the West captivated a generation of readers, and their perspective would remain fanciful until the arrival of Francis Parkman in 1846, who would make them see, in the true sense, in all directions.

Part of Cooper's problem was that he had no access to the work of a talented visual artist on which to base his descriptions. The great work done by George Catlin, Karl Bodmer, and Alfred Miller in the 1830s was not made public until much later. In 1819-20, however, Samuel Seymour accompanied Major Steven Long on an expedition to the Rockies. Handicapped as an artist by a sheer lack of talent, Seymour did not have the tools or the sensibilities to render an accurate, comprehensive view of the West. And so Cooper, who never visited the land beyond the Mississippi, and had no exposure to the next best thing—some perceptive pictures of it—produced the drab landscapes that permeate his major work about the West.

Natty, however, transcends these limitations. In the novel we meet him on the prairies in 1804—the year of Lewis and Clark's outbound journey—encountering a pack of creepy emigrants from Kentucky. Natty is an old man, nearly ninety, but he can still wet his rifle sight and tell a good pilgrim from a varmint. He is a kind of white-haired and sunburnt avatar of the plains, friendly with the Sioux and still resentful of the encroachment of civilization. After a long novel of skirmishes with Indians and moral conflicts and their resolutions, Natty dies in the foothills of the Rockies.

Cooper followed *The Prairie* with *The Pathfinder* (1840) and *The Deerslayer* (1841), two novels that depict events early in Natty's life. James K. Folsom has written that "the combination of the novel of action with the novel of reflection is Cooper's greatest single legacy to the subsequent western story, both philosophically and from the point of view of technique. The problem faced by the author of western tales, then as now, has always been how to assimilate the raw materials of a blood-and-thunder story into a novel of some philosophical respectability."[1]

Following Cooper's lead were other major writers who continued the tradition. Among the early ones was Washington Irving, the beloved creator of Ichabod Crane and Rip Van Winkle. After having spent numerous years in Europe, Irving returned to New York in May 1832, and discovered he was famous. However, he returned with sufficient guilt over being away so long that he bore an aroused earnestness to focus his talents on strictly American themes. He wasted no time.

Along with several colorful companions, Irving toured the Oklahoma prairies for one long eventful and inspirational autumn. Shortly thereafter, Irving returned to his home in New York, his notebooks brimming with observations and sketches from his western tour. For the next two years he shaped this information into a book he titled *A Tour on the Prairies* (1835). It was an enormous success and Irving felt that he had returned to being the American literary lion.

While Irving was organizing his material for the book, he was approached by John Jacob Astor, then seventy, to write a history of Astoria—Astor's ambitious but ill-fated fur trading colony on the Columbia River. The hard-driving Astor promised to put at Irving's disposal all of his journals, records, letters, and documents involving his enterprise, and Astor even hired Irving's nephew, Pierre Monroe Irving, to help the author comb through the wealth of material.

Irving accepted Astor's offer, and while *A Tour on the Prairies* was going to press in April 1835, Irving and his nephew burrowed into paper piles at Astor's fashionable and intimidating mansion at Hell's Gate, New York. In the spacious rooms with a view of the East River through the clerestory windows, Irving and Pierre sifted through Astor's documents and added to them the pioneering insights of Lewis and Clark, Major Steven Long, John Bradbury, and Cooper. Irving also drew heavily on his own recent Western travels and lent to the project his intimate knowledge of buffalo, prairie dogs, Pawnees, Osages, turkey shoots, portages, lost comrades, thunderstorms, and river drainages. This was the knowledge that produced a narrative with rawhide edges and fused the research material into a believable account, distinguishing it from other romantic narratives such as Cooper's *The Prairie*. He finished *Astoria* in two volumes in February 1836, and its appeal further assured Irving that his Southwest foray had been both invigorating and necessary.

As *Astoria* appeared in print, Irving was in Washington on one of his travels from New York. While strolling through the War Department, Irving met Captain Bonneville, who sat at a long table surrounded by Indian artifacts and paintings by Charles Bird King. Bonneville had become famous by journeying to the Rockies in 1832 and simply disappearing. Three years later he showed up at Astor's white-porticoed Hell's Gate, where he encountered Irving as he was engaged in writing *Astoria*. Bonneville's hair-raising adventures in the Rockies were now legion, but the explorer, insecure and self-conscious, could not give voice or shape to them. A master at breathing life into the most dehydrated subjects, Irving made a pact with Bonneville: the author would tell Bonneville's story if the scout made available all his journals relating to the disastrous 1832 trek to the Rockies. The *Adventure of Captain Bonneville* appeared in 1837, the culminating work in Washington Irving's trilogy of western books. Along with Cooper, Irving helped kindle early America's fascination with the West.

By the new decade of the 1840s, however, other writers were heading beyond the Mississippi to continue the tradition. Among these writers were two of note: George Frederick Ruxton and Francis Parkman. Ruxton traveled extensively in the Rockies and Mexico, writing significant works such as *Adventures in Mexico and the Rocky Mountains* (1847) and *Life in the Far West* (1849). Both works captured the color and lifestyles of the mountain men and traders of the West. Parkman's trip to the Rockies and the Santa Fe Trail in 1846 yielded *The Oregon Trail* (1849), best known for its observations of pioneer, Indian, and trapper life.

While the writings of Cooper, Irving, Ruxton, Parkman, and others tended to influence more "serious" literature later on, a new genre appeared in the 1850s that would shape the western romance in the tradition of Zane Grey. In 1854 John Rollin Ridge published *The Life and Adventures of Joaquin Murieta, the Celebrated California Bandit*. Certainly not in the tradition of Cooper or Parkman, Ridge's book imaginatively detailed the colorful escapades of California's Robin Hood thief, thus anticipating a whole body of work extolling outlaws, gunmen, and badmen.

After the Civil War, America was deluged with so-called dime novels, which made famous the exploits of Jesse James, Wild Bill Hickok, Billy the Kid, and the Daltons. Aimed at young readers, the dimes embellished the sordid aspects of the Western frontier and made supermen of ordinary gunslingers and cowpunchers. Beadle and Adams, a leading dime novel publisher, featured many works about notorious badmen. Also belonging to the period were the Harry Castlemon books, which had stirred Grey's imagination as a youngster. An elaborate folklore soon grew up surrounding the "heroes" of the Western frontier, as America created its own versions of Robin Hood, Maid Marian, and the Sheriff of Nottingham from its coterie of marshals and desperadoes.

The book that helped combine the serious approaches to western literature with the more heroic and imaginative versions was Owen Wister's *Virginian* of 1902. One of the great myth-makers of the West, Wister brought respectability to the western novel, even though his characters seem as imposing as those from a Wagnerian opera. This, then, is the tradition—that of Cooper, Irving, Parkman mingled with that of Beadle and Adams, Deadeye Dick, and Wild Bill Hickok, at last congealed in Owen Wister's vigorous book—that forms the background leading up to Zane Grey's arrival. Grey did not seem the likely heir to the role, particularly because his first novels were of the Ohio River Valley during the Revolutionary War. The West of Cooper and Irving and Wister seemed remote indeed—but the time to make his move was near at hand.

꤮

Zane Grey was absolutely enamored of romance writing, and most of his favorite authors wrote in this vein. He was psychologically disposed to it, spending much of his time thinking, writing, acting, and reflecting in a typically romantic fashion. It follows that the study of his work must include some background in the romantic tradition.

In 1851, one of Grey's favorite authors, Nathaniel Hawthorne, included in his preface to *The House of the Seven Gables* the central dilemma of fiction writing as he saw it. He divided imaginative literature into two types, illustrated by what he called the "Novel" and the "Romance." The novel, he explained, targets "a very minute fidelity ... to the probable and ordinary course of man's experience." On the other hand, the romance, although it too must reflect the "truth of the human heart," may "present the truth under circumstances ... of the writer's own choosing or creation." American authors from Cooper, Hawthorne, and Melville forward have successfully integrated the demands of both the novel and the romance with no significant loss of respectability.

As a major narrative form, romance may be viewed as one of the primary types in literature, often dominating the early history of a culture. This is true of Greek, German, and Anglo-Saxon as well as of English medieval literature. In American literature Cooper initiates the romantic viewpoint in the Leatherstocking Tales, thereby setting the stage for the host of real and imaginary heroes of western paperback and hardback fiction.

The major purpose of romance is to realize the desirable. The critic Northrop Frye explains that romance is the form "nearest to wish-fulfillment. . . . The perennially child-like quality of romance is marked by its extraordinary persistent nostalgia, its search for some kind of imaginative golden age in time and space." The accent here is on "wish-fulfillment": the need to seek an imaginary place of safety and desirability, one hopefully removed from the demands and constraints of the real world. In romance, dreams come true, good triumphs over evil, tragedy is transcended, and an ordered world is illustrated by the central character riding into a golden sunset.

The initiation of the hero is central to romance, and most of Zane Grey's protagonists—feeble, diseased, soul-weary—are called upon to test themselves against nature and the forces of evil. They generally arrive in the West from the East with few tools and slim possibilities for success. Only by enduring the crucible (most often a combination of evil characters and the savage desert) can they inherit the serenity and knowledge to live in a healthy, harmonious world.

Another aspect of romance is the hero's journey—the quest—which characterizes several of Grey's best works. The hero must endure a challenging journey, with the reward usually being a maiden, gold, or power. Drawn primarily by his need to rescue someone, the Grey hero encounters numerous obstacles in the course of his noble quest. He may have several helpers, both animal and human, in pursuing his desperate search, such as Mescal's dog in *Heritage of the Desert*, or the Paiute guide Nas Ta Bega in *The Rainbow Trail*, or the nomad Dismukes in *Wanderer of the Wasteland*. Most often in Grey's work, the hero subdues his enemies, wins his rewards, and receives the necessary knowledge and strength required to be a complete man (or woman, in some cases). The so-called "happy ending" is the typical form of romance, compared to the more atypical forms in which the hero dies and descends into the underworld to await rebirth (as in Homer's *Odyssey*).

Although Grey's characters do not attain the stature of other romantic heroes such as Natty Bumppo, Beowulf, Havelok the Dane, Sir Gawain, or Robin Hood, they do share similarities. Jim Lassiter, Bern Venters, and Buck Duane may not be from the misty, sinister forests of Europe or upstate New York, but they operate in much the same way as their predecessors. Inherent in the romantic character's makeup is the need to get things done—usually by himself. He generally trusts no one's judgment but his own. Therefore, Grey's characters take power into their own hands and seek to accomplish what other people cannot.

In choosing his literary path Zane Grey early on seized the trappings of romance. His ultimate wish-fulfillment was to be part of his own narratives, to experience the joys and struggles of his characters in a bygone age, and to eliminate as much as possible his involvement with the present moment. Grey also drank deeply of the western tradition in literature; similarly, he mixed in his own brand of romance and description, creating a unique view of a West that was already slipping into history.

The Muse Is Heard

New York in spring 1903 was a city suspended in a delirious daydream. With its teeming streets and honking tempos, its horseless carriages competing with horse-drawn milk buggies, it was a city undergoing dramatic changes. Huge armies of immigrants swarmed on the docks and soon spread out all over town, adding to the babble of voices that already resounded in the back streets and byways. Broadway and Wall Street were crowded; dirt, decay, and crime stalked the Lower East Side, while fashionable avenues near Central Park exposed their wrought iron balconies and tall French windows to the smirched sunlight.

This was the civilized wilderness that Zane Grey had endured for close to seven long years. More and more he associated the city, any city, with effeminacy, corruption, and weakness, while he praised pristine nature as the citadel of morality, strength, and manliness.

With Dolly encouraging him through the winter and spring of 1903, Grey wrote the final chapters of his first novel. Every page, sometimes every word, tormented him, as he endured the wild-bull ride that every writer takes with his first novel. He desperately wanted it to succeed and be published. He had no expectation, nor even the remotest thought, that he was about to inherit a tradition.

He showed everything he had written to Dolly on a weekly basis. She recognized his narrative skill and clumsy grammar, but she withheld criticism. Unsure of himself, Grey sought her approval at every turn. She became his chief emotional supporter during the spells when his confidence in himself was flagging. Grey's self-esteem was always tenuous and held in prison by authority figures such as his parents. Dolly broke through this captivity and emerged not only as a talented literary assistant but also as an emotional rallier as well. She painstakingly copied Grey's scrawl into the final version he would show to publishers.

A first novelist not only wears his heart on his sleeve but also cradles it tenderly in his hands and presents it for the whole world to regard. It was no different with Zane Grey. He thought that his creation was the greatest thing—the only thing—on earth. When Dolly had finished copying it, he bundled it up and took it to Harper and Brothers in Manhattan. The title page read: *"Betty Zane* by P. Zane Grey. Cover design, letters, and illustrations by the author." After it was rejected, Grey was plunged into despair. Dolly encouraged him to submit it to other publishers. Angry and in shock, he shepherded the *Betty Zane* manuscript around New York City. One publisher after another refused it. Grey sank into depression, listening to all the critical voices from childhood forward that played ceaselessly in his mind.[1]

Unable to bear seeing Grey flounder in despair, Dolly intervened in the summer of 1903. She offered to give Zane the money to have the book self-published. Grey at first refused, but Dolly persuaded him to accept her offer. Grey took his manuscript to the Charles Francis Press, where it was printed. And so Zane Grey became a first novelist and joined the ranks of other prominent artists like Walt Whitman who self-published their initial work. The sight of this work in print, indeed in his hands, uplifted Grey and he launched a furious publicity campaign for *Betty Zane.* Distributing copies to local bookstores and mailing out several books to reviewers, he proceeded to cover the known literary territory single-handedly. For several months he tramped the New York sidewalks, coercing bookstore owners into prominently displaying his book. He sent copies to his dental patients and to the folks and family in Zanesville. Grey was an ecstatic boy again, an author with his first book in print and about to scale the initial heights of literary fame.[2]

Although the sales of *Betty Zane* were minimal and generally limited to the New York area, Grey's confidence soared. He remained embarrassed, however, by Dolly's role in its publication. He referred to his benefactor as simply "a wealthy patient."[3] *Betty Zane* would never earn back the money Grey sank into it. But it didn't make a difference: its appearance was a clear signal to him that he had arrived as an author.

Betty Zane tells the story of the Zanes and their friends as they attempt to carve a living out of the raw wilderness of the Ohio River Valley. James Fenimore Cooper's influence is evident virtually everywhere: in the Indian-white relationships, and in the descriptions of the extensive wilderness, a wilderness that both threatens the existence of the settlers and insulates them from the hostile Indian tribes surrounding their rudimentary fort.

Despite its derivative phrases and clumsy transitions between exposition and description, *Betty Zane* is a charming and gracefully written first novel. What is significant is not what Grey put in—and he put in a good deal—but what he left out. The customary flaws of first novels—purple descriptive prose, stock characters, starched dialogue, and excessive adjectives—are absent here. Moreover, by virtue of Grey's obvious passion for his subject, the idiosyncrasies of his ancestors' lives are beautifully told and sparely described. After all, the Zanes, Lew Wetzel, and Simon Girty were real people, and Grey does a superb job of giving them distinct voices and characteristics.

Why publisher after publisher refused *Betty Zane* is one of the mysteries of the business. Perhaps the editors thought it was difficult to market to an adult audience. Certainly the frontier life of early America appealed to a wide readership. A contemporary of Grey, Joseph Altsheler, created a highly successful career by writing of the pioneer life in Kentucky and the Ohio River Valley during the same period as the Zanes. Altsheler may have succeeded where Zane Grey languished by targeting a young adult audience. Altsheler's Young Trailer series, published by Appleton-Century, brought him quick and enduring fame among young boys.

Perhaps the most memorable character in *Betty Zane* is Lew Wetzel. Solid and taciturn, Wetzel becomes the prototype of the Grey hero, who after some brief encounters with civilization turns away to embrace the life of forest, mountain, or desert. After his family is murdered by Indians, Wetzel, or "Deathwind" as he is known, becomes a ruthless stalker of Shawnee, Huron, and Delaware alike. Wetzel is consumed by his obsession for hunting and killing Indians. He does, however, return to Fort Henry periodically to bring fresh venison and to flirt with Betty Zane. He is threatened by Betty's affection for him, and ultimately he allows Betty to select Alfred Clarke, a man more suited to Betty's need for domestic comfort.

As the reader can quickly discover, Grey reveres Wetzel as a hunter, woodsman, and white "knower" of the wilderness. But the author gives his hero several human touches that help raise him above a mere killer of Indians. For instance, Lew Wetzel is quite proud of his long dark hair (which hangs below his knees when combed out), and, before shooting at a target, he raises a generous lock of it to the breeze to ascertain its direction. Or, in a moment of passion for Betty Zane, he dances with her at a social event at Fort Henry. The contrast between the tall buckskinned frontiersman and the petite Betty Zane is nicely rendered by Grey and helps smooth the edges of Wetzel's stoic character.

Alan Hodge, a fine translator of Maupassant, once remarked that "often there is a fine bloom about a first novel which its writer never quite achieves again, however more expert he becomes in technique or more nearly universal in his sympathies." This is essentially true of *Betty Zane*. Its remarkable charm and spirit, its believable evocation of an age, give it a luster that sets it apart from the more complex and technically better sequels, *Spirit of the Border* and *The Last Trail*. Alfred Clarke and Isaac Zane, tough, young, and naive, rise to moments of personal bravery. Col. Zane, who had claimed "tomahawk possession" of the valley, strides forth with compassion and a conviction that neither the British nor the Indians shall wrest the valley from the settlers.

> A man can die. He is glorious when he calmly accepts death; but when he fights like a tiger, when he stands at bay his back to the wall, a broken weapon in his hand, bloody, defiant, game to the end, then he is sublime. Then he wrings respect from the souls of even his bitterest foes. Then he is avenged even in his death. (p. 268)

Betty Zane, however, is the life force of the novel. To the question, "What can women do in times of war?" Grey supplies the answer, "They help, they cheer, they inspire, and if their cause is lost they must accept death or worse. Few women have the courage for self-destruction." Betty Zane is one of those rare exceptions. As the story reaches its dramatic peak with the attack on the fort, Silas Zane and his dwindling forces within the block-house face almost certain death:

> No wonder Silas Zane and his men weakened in that moment. With only a few charges for their rifles and none for the cannon how could they hope to hold out against the savages? Alone they could have drawn their tomahawks and have made a dash through the lines of Indians, but with the women and the children that was impossible.
>
> "Wetzel, what can we do? For God's sake, advise us!" said Silas hoarsely. "We cannot hold the Fort without powder. We cannot leave the women here. We had better tomahawk every woman in the block-house than let her fall into the hands of Girty."
>
> "Send some one fer powder," answered Wetzel.
>
> "Do you think it possible," said Silas quickly, a ray of hope lighting up his haggard features. "There's plenty of powder in Eb's cabin. Whom shall we send? Who will volunteer?"
>
> Three men stepped forward, and others made a movement.
>
> "They'd plug a man full of lead afore he'd get ten foot from the gate," said Wetzel. "I'd go myself, but it wouldn't do no good. Send a boy, and one as can run like a streak."
>
> "There are no lads big enough to carry a keg of powder. Harry Bennet might go," said Silas. "How is he, Bessie?"

"He's dead," answered Mrs. Zane.

Wetzel made a motion with his hands and turned away. A short, intense silence followed this indication of hopelessness from him. The women understood, for some of them covered their faces, while others sobbed.

"*I will go.*"

It was Betty's voice, and it rang clear and vibrant throughout the room. (pp. 268–69)

While Wetzel represents silent, durable manhood, Betty Zane embodies the qualities of spirit, independence, and fidelity that Grey cherished in women. Early in the novel Betty implores her friend Alfred Clarke to stay the course: " 'You are unhappy. Try to rise above it. Who knows what will befall this little settlement? It may be swept away by the savages or it may grow to be a mighty city. It must take that chance. So must you, so must we all take chances. You are here. Find your work and do it cheerfully, honestly, and let the future take care of itself . . .' " In a different context, this passage reads like Dolly encouraging Grey to stick with his writing no matter what the obstacles.

Betty Zane is straightforward, youthful romance, with no pretensions to emulating Cooper or challenging Owen Wister. It is a good book without being a great book. It shows Zane Grey's developing sense of creating character, writing description, and establishing a coherent narrative. If nothing else it launches the author to the next step in the important process of becoming a writer, with a few lessons learned and several *faux pas* avoided.

While *Betty Zane* was in bookstores, Grey began work on his second novel, *Spirit of the Border,* which told of the exploits of his great-great-uncle Jonathan Zane and more of the adventures of the implacable Lew Wetzel. Although his first novel sold modestly, it helped gear him for the writing life. And so by the middle of 1904, with *Spirit* in full creative swing, Grey was painstakingly at work on his craft.

His diary entries reveal that he was consciously trying to develop a literary code. He believed that attentive, thorough reading was essential for a writer, underlining that a book should be read "slowly, repeatedly, carefully . . . until [the reader is] imbued with the power and thought of the writer." Consequently, he turned to his favorite authors for sustenance: Hugo, Stevenson, Tennyson, Hawthorne, and Wordsworth. Of Hawthorne he wrote: "his sadness, his melancholy, his dreams are mine."[4]

Realizing that writing was a precise, architectural system, Grey provided his deliberate views on sentence structure: "Think what the sentence is to exist for—what is its central thought. Do not change subjects if it can be helped. . . . Cut out intensive expression and superlatives that are unnecessary. Beware of 'but', 'it', and 'there.' Cut them out when possible. . . . Work for clearness, sequence, climax. . . . Brevity helps action and makes strength and force."[5]

Also in 1904, at Dolly's insistence, Grey began keeping a notebook, in which he dissected the world around him. Human nature intrigued him, and he wrote: "The author must so thoroughly understand human nature that he will know exactly what and how great a motive is necessary for a certain act of a certain person. . . . The great gift of a writer is sincerity. A writer must have strong and noble convictions about life."[6]

Although his understanding of human psychology was severely limited, Grey did excel at description almost from his first novel. He wrote that "a cunning writer will avail himself of images likely to be stored in the minds of his readers; with appeal to the emotions, to the general experiences of mankind."[7] He believed that effective description proceeded from simple to complex imagery, and that a writer should provide an initial dominant impression.

Grey finished *Spirit of the Border* in fall 1904. He realized that it was a better novel stylistically than *Betty Zane*. Buoyed by his rising confidence and Dolly's emotional support, he delivered the manuscript to the offices of Harper and Brothers. Again, it came back in the plain brown mailer that had accompanied his submission. And again, Grey despaired.

He resumed the frustrating routine of sending out the manuscript to other publishers, having it return like some fearless homing pigeon.

While this agonizing process continued, he began writing his third novel of the Ohio River trilogy, *The Last Trail*. Grey worked on it through the winter of 1904 and into the spring of 1905. He got bolder in *Spirit of the Border* and *The Last Trail*, aiming for a more adult audience by raising the level of violence and by eliminating most of the sentimental references. When the third book was copied by Dolly into legible script, he sent it to Harper's—and it quickly came back with the standard rejection slip. Grey seemed intent on having Harper's publish his books, and even five years later this intent had become a passion and somewhat of an obsession.

Although the Ohio River novels achieved little commercial success, Grey derived great satisfaction from relating the adventures and exploits of his eighteenth-century ancestors. Betty Zane, Ebenezer Zane, Jonathan Zane, and Lew Wetzel return in *The Last Trail* to make Fort Henry a safe haven on the western frontier. Grey's narrative focus shifts to Jonathan Zane and his romance with Helen Sheppard. A lifelong woodsman and hunter, Jonathan falls victim to the charms of the worldly Helen. At the time of the writing of *The Last Trail*, Grey was a thirty-three-year-old bachelor deeply in love with Dolly; the parallels with his forest heroes are all too apparent. Jonathan Zane—like others of Grey's protagonists—is a heroic version of Grey himself.

In *The Last Trail*, Jonathan joins forces with Lew Wetzel in a final, dangerous mission against the Indians. Helen Sheppard, however, proves to be a more serious obstacle for Jonathan than the Shawnees or the wilderness. In one scene Jonathan and Helen are alone in the forest; the weary Helen leans her head on Jonathan's shoulder and falls asleep:

> The borderman trembled. The sudden nestling of her head against him, the light caress of her fragrant hair across his cheek, revived a sweet, almost-conquered, almost-forgotten emotion. He felt an inexplicable thrill vibrate through him. No untrodden, ambushed wild, no perilous trail, no dark and bloody encounter had ever made him feel fear as had the kiss of this maiden. He had sternly silenced faint, unfamiliar, yet tender, voices whispering in his heart; and now his rigorous discipline was as if it were not, for at her touch he trembled. . . .

Then honesty demanded that he probe his own feelings. Sternly, as if judging a renegade, he searched out in his simple way the truth.... Love he had never believed could be possible for him....

No, he was no longer indifferent. As surely as those pale stars blinked far above, he knew the delight of a woman's presence. It moved him to study the emotion, as he studied all things, which was the habit of his borderman's life. Did it come from knowledge of her beauty, matchless as that of the mountain-laurel? ... Beauty was wonderful, but not everything. Beauty belonged to her, but she would have been irresistible without it. Was it not because she was a woman? That was the secret. She was a woman with all a woman's charm to bewitch, to twine round the strength of men as the ivy encircles the oak; with all a woman's weakness to pity and to guard; with all a woman's wilful burning love, and with all a woman's mystery.

At last so much of life was intelligible to him. The renegade committed his worst crimes because even in his outlawed, homeless state, he could not exist without the companionship, if not the love, of a woman. The pioneer's toil and privation were for a woman, and the joy of loving her and living for her.... All nature sang that love made life worth living. Love, then, was everything. (pp. 123–25)

With two book manuscripts circulating in New York City, Grey retreated into the Pennsylvania countryside to consider purchasing a five-acre tract of land at the convergence of the Delaware and Lackawaxen rivers. A two-level cottage stood on the far end of the property surveying the forest and the broad curves of the rivers. It was a fisherman's bonanza. Grey loved it immediately, and with his family's financial backing, bought it with what dwindling financial reserves he had. Dolly's inheritance from her grandfather would help to supplement their income after their marriage.

Meanwhile, A. L. Burt Company, mainly a reprint publishing house but later to publish such authors as Edgar Rice Burroughs and Rex Beach, purchased *Spirit of the Border.* They refused to pay Zane in advance, but did promise him royalties after publication.

Although Grey had decided as early as 1904 to renounce dentistry and assume writing full-time, he unequivocally resolved to do so in summer of 1905 with the contract on *Spirit of the Border.*[8] In late summer and early fall he closed his practice in New York, bundled up his belongings and notebooks, and headed to peaceful routines at his newly purchased cottage in Lackawaxen. His departure from New York was swift and dramatic, and he relished the divorce from the big city.

As the distance between Zane at Lackawaxen and Dolly in New York began to wear on the couple, their letters assumed a more urgent and passionate note. They were to be married in November and they planned to settle afterwards at Lackawaxen while Grey pursued his literary career. In September 1905 he was writing his fourth book, *Lethe*.[9] This book was to be a radical departure from the Ohio woods of the eighteenth century, and from an exchange of letters between Dolly and Zane one can see the difficulty Grey was having finding the proper voice for the novel. The first paragraph as he originally penned it reads:

> Folly, thou has cost me dear; the light of woman's eye—Ah! Wine—thou mocker! Outcast am I, thrown from my father's house hard upon the world, after an idle, luxurious, improvident youth. Better surely, to yield to the strain of suicide blood in me and seek forgetfulness in the embrace of cold dark death. What makes life worth living? Indefinable, for me, as the unpardonable sin. Yet to give it up, at twenty-five, when the blood burns, for the unknown—No. I will see this game of life out to its bitter end. I will try again, and yet again. Men may rise on stepping stones of their dead selves to higher things.[10]

Unable to find a suitable literary voice, Grey resorts to a little mock Hamlet—or mock Byron at his worst. The narrator seems as confused as Grey is by his sudden departure from historical fiction.

On September 4, 1905, Grey wrote Dolly about the opening of *Lethe:* "I enclose a paragraph [above] I want you to *study* in view of making it the opening for my novel *Lethe*. I woke up in the night, and the words came out almost as you have them." Note that Grey underlined the word "study." Since most of the paragraph is undecipherable, Dolly must have been confused as to where Grey was going with it. She responded to the paragraph in a letter in mid-September 1905: "I fail to

The Grey home at Lackawaxen, Pennsylvania, c. 1910. About thirty miles east of Scranton, Lackawaxen provided a peaceful alternative to Zane's dental practice in New York City. Here Zane Grey wrote *The Heritage of the Desert* and *Riders of the Purple Sage,* among other works. *Courtesy of the G. M. Farley Collection, Hagerstown, Maryland*

understand such hieroglyphics. . . . What can you possibly mean? Perhaps in the long while that we have been parted you have bent your energies to acquiring some new language."[11] Alas, the original concept for *Lethe* was never completed, which may have saved Grey further frustration and embarrassment, because it was simply unpublishable.

Grey took the time away from his furious writing schedule to marry Dolly on the twenty-first of November 1905 in New York City, when he temporarily surrendered to the wild throb and hectic pace of a town he severely loathed so that he could marry the woman he deeply loved. He was thirty-three and she was twenty-two.

These formative years between 1902 and 1905 were crucial ones for Grey. He had shed the role prescribed for him by his father. He became engaged to and eventually married the woman he loved. He began—

Dolly Grey, the former Lina Elise Roth, at the cottage at Lackawaxen, c. 1905. Mrs. Zane Grey was her husband's editor, typist, and major fan. She also helped him finance his first book, *Betty Zane,* in 1903. *Courtesy of the G. M. Farley Collection, Hagerstown, Maryland*

very slowly at first but with ever increasing momentum—his career as a writer. He could have stopped with the modest success of *Betty Zane* and a few magazine stories. However, the prospect of returning to dentistry and the lure of a few minor successes drove him on.

Dolly, of course, was instrumental. Without her talents as editor and copyist, he may have been likely to give up hope during those gloomy years. She saw him through failure, acute depression, more failure, brief success, and recognized when his talent was on a dangerous course.

Although the years 1902–1905 yielded no great work, they provided fertile ground and disciplined understanding for the struggle to follow. Most importantly, he had begun to formulate the ideas and perceptions that would make him a writer. He began keeping a notebook and logging his observations. He developed, perhaps too rigidly, his views on grammar, syntax, and style. In many ways they were bitter years with a sprinkling of minor triumphs; but they were necessary years of learning, fumbling and lingering in windy darkness.

El Dorado

By January 12, 1906, the New York–Chicago Number 3 was whisking Zane and Dolly over the wide farmlands and wooded rises of Ohio. They were on their honeymoon, bound for California.

They caught the California Limited in Chicago and proceeded onto the plains of Kansas and then into the empty grasslands of New Mexico. On January 15 they arrived at El Tovar Hotel overlooking the Grand Canyon. That night they joined a flock of pilgrims to behold the glory of the canyon at sunset, Dolly noting in her diary that the sight was "a second inferno, stupendous, awe inspiring, glowing with fiery colors."[1]

The next day they took the required packtrain excursion down into the mouth of the canyon. The eastern tenderfoots were aghast all the way down as the yawning chasm opened up, revealing its stark, vivid colors and ragged spurs of rock. Snow covered the canyon floor and dribbled onto the exposed shoulders of stone.

All the while, Grey absorbed this serrated and pillared landscape of the desert. He was strongly attracted to the desert from the beginning, warmed by the great aloneness, the sparse variety of plant life, and the prospect of a direct connection to nature and time. The sky was different here: austere, vacant, eternal. During this first trip to the desert, Grey began to develop as deep a love for the landforms of the West as he harbored for the woods and streams of Pennsylvania and New York. His feelings about the desert in 1906 were urgent and young, but without conviction. They would develop in later years as he returned repeatedly to witness the silent, sere landscape.

They left the Grand Canyon and continued on to southern California, which in the early 1900s had the look of an Italian garden with lemon and orange groves parading neatly to the sea. After visiting Los Angeles, they took a trolley south to San Diego, passing sheep grazing on the coastal hills. Zane got his first taste of sea fishing in San Diego, and even caught a shark on one of his first attempts. While Dolly lounged and read, Grey spent several days fishing on the pier.

By early February they were on Catalina Island, off the coast from Los Angeles. Grey recognized the fishing possibilities of this West Coast paradise, but with his limited income was unable to take advantage of them. He did dream, however.

The honeymoon had been relaxing and stimulating for both Zane and Dolly. It had opened a whole new landscape for Grey, and by the time they returned to Lackawaxen, he had also resumed his demanding writing schedule.

The areas of land that Zane Grey had glimpsed—north of the Grand Canyon and just beyond the Utah border—were regions of abrupt contrasts, pure colors, lurid beauty, and fierce rivalries. This landscape was to be the setting for numerous later novels, and its skies and sands would figure prominently in his descriptions of the West.[2] He had seen the land only briefly on his honeymoon, but fate would bring him back.

The wind-racked and sun-pummeled strip of land was far removed from twentieth-century civilization and seemed older than time. To the east was the Painted Desert; to the north the Kanab desert; to the west the Virgin Mountains; and to the south the San Francisco Peaks. The mighty, muddy Colorado swept through the land, carving its deep scar through the forests and canyons where mountain lion, bear, deer, and wild horses competed for survival. Pine, cedar, and juniper dug their shallow roots into the soil and struggled with drought and flood.

This area, known as the Arizona Strip, had been Mormon country since the 1870s and 1880s. Numerous settlements dotted the canyon country on both sides of the Arizona-Utah border. Since the border region was primitive and remote, several Mormons regarded northern Arizona as part of Mormon Utah and settled there.[3]

The Colorado River crossing at Lee's Ferry, some ten miles from the border, was administered by Jim Emmett, a tall Moses-like figure with a great mane of gray hair and ponderous eyes. A polygamist, Emmett worked the land alongside his wives and children. His cattle shared the grazing land around Lee's Ferry with the herd of another unique personality, Charles Jesse "Buffalo" Jones.

Jones was small and wiry with gray-blue eyes. In his embroidered buckskins and leather chaps, he looked as if he had come straight from a buffalo hunt of the 1850s. Jones had been a bison hunter and a warden in Yellowstone; more recently he had dedicated his life to saving and protecting the buffalo. On his ranch in northern Arizona he was experimenting with the hybridization of buffalo and cattle, intent on creating a breed that would flourish in the harsh desert environment. His "cattalo" experiment was just getting started, but like most fresh ventures it needed boosts of financial support from the outside.

Jim Emmett's influence on Zane Grey will be discussed shortly, but Buffalo Jones's impact came first and its effect on the young author was deep and enduring. Jones had traveled to New York in early 1907, ostensibly to lecture eastern audiences about his various western exploits and to woo support for his experiments. His lusty tales ranged from roping mountain lions in the Grand Canyon to capturing bears in Yellowstone. Jones was bold, assertive, and knowledgeable about the vanishing West, the perfect mentor to tutor the young Grey. In fact, Jones was the second significant male teacher to enter Grey's life (Muddy Miser being the first and Jim Emmett the third).[4]

In New York to attend Jones's presentation, Grey had come through a difficult year of writing. *The Last Trail* still had not found a publisher and Grey was worrying about it. He did manage to sell fishing articles to *Shield's Magazine* and a four-page angling story and baseball article to *Field and Stream. Spirit of the Border* had been out for two years and was selling modestly. After nearly five years of intense writing, Grey could boast only two published novels (one self-published) and a handful of magazine articles.

Although Jones delivered an inspired lecture that spring evening, it met with a disastrous response from the audience. At key points in Jones's delivery, several vocal members in the crowd hissed and catcalled; others walked out, apparently disgusted with Jones's unbelievable yarns. Grey was accompanied at the lecture by Alvah James, a noted South American explorer he had met at the Campfire Club in New York.[5] After the presentation Grey asked James to introduce him to the aging plainsman.[6]

Alvah James brought the two together, Grey shaking Jones's gloved hand. At this point in his career Grey was casting about in his mind for new material to replace the sagas of Lew Wetzel, Jonathan Zane, and Simon Girty. In Buffalo Jones Grey saw the embodiment of western folklore and history—a hero of much the same stature as Betty Zane.

Later, Grey visited Jones at his hotel. The cantankerous hunter was bitter over his treatment by the audience, and Grey was quick to offer his support and sympathy. He also proposed to accompany Jones to Arizona and write about their experiences, thereby providing finances for Jones's experiments with cattle and buffalo.

Because Jones was unconvinced of Grey's writing talent, the author left him a copy of *Betty Zane.*[7] Two days later the enthusiastic Jones clasped Grey's shoulder with a brawny hand and snapped: "Where'd you learn to write like that?" Jones added that he would like it very much if Zane Grey would accompany him to his ranch in Arizona.

At first Grey was hesitant about the venture, particularly because it meant coming up with expenses from the last of Dolly's inheritance. Dolly, however, insisted that he go, telling him it would be unfair to Colonel Jones to back out, and encouraging him not to worry about her. She had a hunch that this trip to the West would be the turning point in his career.[8] Somewhat sheepishly, Grey agreed. However, he felt ashamed about allowing his wife to finance the trip, and moreover, about leaving her just over a year after their marriage to go on what amounted to an extended bachelor party in Arizona. His letters to her from the desert are invariably signed "Pearl," indicating a certain boyish, and perhaps guilty, attitude he harbored about the trip.

By late March 1907 he was headed to Arizona by rail. When he got to the Grand Canyon on March 27 he wrote Dolly that he had "arrived in a blinding blizzard. The hotel [the El Tovar] is crowded, and me in my tough clothes. Dear, your two letters broke me all up. I am sick and wish I were home with you. . . . Your letters were splendid but they made me unhappy. I know I shall come back to you loving you more than ever . . ."[9]

Grey traveled south to Flagstaff to join Jim Emmett, his two sons, Buffalo Jones, and two men hired by Emmett. Their plan was to head north to Jones's ranch and then explore the area in and around the Grand Canyon. All in the party, except Grey, were Mormons. Grey was curious to learn more about Mormonism, and particularly about its followers. After he briefly met the group he was going to travel with, he confided to Dolly in a letter: "We shall start in a day or two. We travel with the Mormons for a hundred and eighty miles. I'll get to study them and get to go into the Moki and Indian towns. This ought to make great material for the occasional short story I want to write."[10] Four days later, still in Flagstaff waiting for a Californian named Wallace to join them, he again wrote Dolly that the Mormon group was "a tough bunch. They all pack guns. But they're nice fellows."[11]

Buffalo Jones soon decided that they should leave without Wallace, and Emmett agreed. Soon the pack mules were loaded and several rowdy, barking dogs joined the caravan. Marshaling the elements into a semi-organized group, the men swung onto their horses, including Grey, who had not ridden since leaving Ohio.[12]

Traveling north they plodded through the dense pine forests below the San Francisco Peaks.[13] Grey clung desperately to his saddle, the pain in his muscles and joints aggravated by every movement of his horse. After the Mormons found a camping spot, some twenty-five miles north of Flagstaff, Grey gingerly climbed down from his mount, ate supper, and groaned himself to sleep in his blankets.[14]

The morning sun revealed the undulating sands, the ragged lava rock spurs, and the sagebrush stretching far to the north, past the Wapatki Indian ruins, the Little Colorado River, the Moenkopi Wash, and the severe ochre walls of Echo Cliffs. The sand was deep sienna-red against the rich blue sky. Through this landscape they made their way, heading to the Little Colorado River.

As they moved into the Painted Desert, Grey was overcome with passion and mute with subdued joy. "Imagination had pictured the desert for me as a vast, sandy plain, flat and monotonous," he wrote. "Reality showed me desolate mountains gleaming bare in the sun, long lines of red bluffs, white sand dunes . . . fading all around into the purple haze of the deceiving distance." The air, too, "carried a languor, a dreaminess, tidings of far-off things, an enthralling promise. The fragrance of flowers, the beauty and grace of women, the sweetness of music, the mystery of life—all seemed to float on that promise. It was the air breathed by the lotus-eaters, when they dreamed and wandered no more."[15]

For the next several weeks, as they pushed farther north to the big Colorado and wandered through the Grand Canyon and the Kaibab forests where they hunted mountain lions, Grey patiently sponged up this alien but compelling lifestyle. He attached words to the strange landforms and striking colors he saw; he weighed and absorbed the men's bizarre lingo; he watched as they broke camp, doused the fire with their coffee, saddled their horses, tested each other's machismo, and rode as part of a disheveled caravan under the lordly sun and piercing blue sky.

Moreover, he came to know men on an emotionally intimate level—perhaps for the first time in his life. From the sixty-three-year-old Buffalo Jones he learned desert and Indian lore, and additionally, how to survive in a harsh, desolate environment. From Jim Emmett he learned Mormon culture and folkways. Even though Grey loathed polygamy he could, through Emmett, begin to appreciate the positive aspects of Mormonism.(Grey particularly sympathized with Mormon women, whom Lassiter in *Riders of the Purple Sage* called "the blindest, unhappiest women on earth."[16]) The spirit of Buffalo Jones was to appear in several later Grey novels, and the shadow of Jim Emmett stretched across the pages of *Heritage of the Desert* as the figure of August Naab, the stoic, patriarchal Mormon tutor of easterner John Hare. Grey would say of Emmett that he "endured loneliness, hunger, thirst . . . the fierce sandstorm, the desert blizzard, poverty, labor without help, illness without medicine, tasks without remuneration, no comfort, but little sleep, so few of the joys commonly yearned for by men, and pain, pain, always some kind of pain."[17]

Jim Emmett also supplied Grey with the gift of silent observation. "Surely, of all the gifts that have come to me from contact with the West," wrote Grey, "this one of sheer love of wilderness, beauty, color, grandeur, has been the greatest, the most significant for my work."[18]

When *The Last of the Plainsmen,* Grey's book detailing his travels with Buffalo Jones and Jim Emmett, was published in 1908, its very appearance was something of a curiosity.

Predictably, Grey had raced back to Lackawaxen from Arizona in the late spring of 1907 burning to write of his desert exploits. Buffalo Jones had corresponded with the Greys, eagerly anticipating the completion of the manuscript. When the book was finished, Grey had Buffalo Jones read it. The plainsman was impressed with and enthusiastic about Grey's creation. With their confidence soaring, Grey and Jones left the cottage at Lackawaxen and headed to New York City. There they were to meet Harper and Brothers editor Ripley Hitchcock, whom Jones knew.

Harper's had rejected all three of his previous novels, but Grey was convinced that they would not pass on *The Last of the Plainsmen*. Grey left the manuscript with Hitchcock. After several days' deliberation, Hitchcock stood across the desk from Zane Grey and spoke the words that hammered at Grey's soul. "I do not see anything in this to convince me you can write either narrative or fiction." To Grey, these words aggravated a wound already opened by his father when he was fifteen and made to fester by countless subsequent rejections. Stunned and hurt, he struggled to get out of Hitchcock's office and down the stairs. Once on the sidewalk, he grabbed a lamppost and barely averted a tumble onto the pavement. He managed to get the train back to Lackawaxen, where he collected his thoughts and emotions. Several days later he stonily committed himself once again to the writing life. "Suddenly," he later wrote, "something marvelous happened to me, in my mind, to my eyesight, to my breast. That moment should logically have been the end of my literary aspirations! From every point of view I seemed lost. But someone inside me cried out: 'He does not know. *They* are all wrong!'"[19]

The Last of the Plainsmen was published several months later by the Outing Publishing Company, a minor publishing firm dealing in books for sportsmen. It had been rejected by other major publishers and Outing picked it up with the agreement that they would not pay Grey a penny for it until it went into a second printing.

The Last of the Plainsmen certainly did not deserve the treatment it received. It is a sound book—one of Grey's best early works—and one brimming with vigor and movement. The literature of the West is filled with the various exploits of greenhorns encountering the rugged outdoors. Irving, Parkman, Ruxton, and Teddy Roosevelt, to name a few, made their reputations in such works. Grey's book falls into this genre. It does not have the high seriousness of Parkman's work or any of the sustained description of mountain life in Ruxton, but it is a lighthearted introduction to Western frontier life.

The title itself bears examining. It seems that Grey wished to pay homage to Fenimore Cooper, hence his variation on the name *Last of the Mohicans*. Although Buffalo Jones and Zane both agreed on the appropriateness of *Last of the Plainsmen*, the title may have been responsible for the initial failure of the book. Jones, of course, was known to a segment of the population, but in no way could most people recognize him from the title, or for that matter throughout the text. A more strategic choice of title might have capitalized on the trip itself. In any event, *Last of the Plainsmen* stuck, but it is one of the less imaginative titles in Grey's collection.

Originally the book was to focus on Jones's experiments with cattle and buffalo, but Grey shifted the emphasis to the more colorful, action-oriented activities surrounding the stalking of mountain lions. Buffalo Jones emerges as a forceful character, with Grey providing several good asides about Jones's extensive career. One of these is the plainsman's hilarious attempt to catch a musk-ox in the arctic. Also surfacing is Grey's characterization of the hunter-turned-conservationist as a mystic and dreamer, a man benevolently trying to preserve many vanishing species of wildlife. Grey describes Jones's "inscrutable face . . . keen eyes, half closed from years of searching the wide plains. . . . A strange stillness enfold[ing] his features—the tranquility earned from a long life of adventure."

In finding the American West Grey came into his own as a writer of description. His apprehension of the desert atmosphere is acute and shows flashes of Joseph Conrad: "the scaly red ground descended gradually; bare red knolls, like waves, rolled away northward; black buttes reared their flat heads; long ranges of sand flowed between them like streams, all sloped away to merge into gray, shadowy obscurity, into wild and desolate, dreamy and misty nothingness."[20] Or, when Grey's party reaches the Colorado River, he realizes he is in the presence of a raging animal:

> To look at the river was to court terror, but I had to look. It was an infernal thing. It roared in hollow, sullen voice, as a monster growling. It had a voice, this river, and one strangely changeful. It moaned as if in pain—it whined, it cried. Then at times it would seem strangely silent. The current was complex and mutable as human life. It boiled, beat

and bulged. The bulge itself was an incomprehensible thing, like the roaring life of the waters from a submarine explosion. Then it would smooth out and run like oil. . . . Again it swelled near the boat, in great, boiling, hissing eddies.[21]

One flaw in Grey's writing, however, is his inability to sustain vivid description beyond the thumbnail variety. Sometimes the most enthralling descriptive moments could be raised to greater importance if Grey developed and focused more. Conrad could suffuse an entire story in atmosphere, but Grey, still the student, develops it only briefly—if gorgeously.

After all is said and done, Grey had a greater affinity with Conrad than with any other contemporary writer. Both were concerned with morality and behavior in the most remote places and under the most difficult circumstances. Grey chose the desert to temper and mold his characters; Conrad selected the sea because he believed it helped reveal people's essential selves.

Both Grey and Conrad favored primitive and secluded locations as vehicles for their characters' spiritual redemption. Both were romantics who were obsessed with the horizon; both were dreamers in the true sense of the word, who sent their characters into far-flung deserts, villages, outposts, and unknown waters to grapple with their own drifting souls. Passages by Grey, such as his further description of the river, echo Conrad: "I looked upstream to see the stupendous granite walls separated in a gigantic split that must have been made by a terrible seismic disturbance; and from this gap poured the dark, turgid, mystic flood."

When it came to writing about the desert of the American West, Grey could, initially, hold his own with anybody. In the later novels, however, his descriptions frequently lose their power simply because they are exhausted from use, and his adjectives and nouns sound more like formulas pulled from an available grab bag than eloquent evocations spun from direct observation. But in the handful of early novels of the West, roughly between 1908 and 1920, his heightened receptivity to the desert translates into sharp, even compelling, literary description. For instance, the Grand Canyon in *Last of the Plainsmen* is transformed into a great, mythical, unearthly landscape:

> The sun, a liquid red globe, had just touched its underside to the pink cliffs of Utah, and fired a crimson flood of light over the wonderful mountains, plateaus, escarpments, mesas, domes and turrets of the gorge. The rim wall of Powell's Plateau was a thin streak of fire; the timber above like grass of gold; and the long slopes below shaded from bright to dark. Point Sublime, bold and bare, ran out toward the plateau, jealously reaching for the sun. Bass's Tomb peeped over the Saddle. The Temple of Vishnu lay bathed in vapory shading clouds, and Shinumo Altar shone with rays of glory.[22]

It is this silent energy behind the visual splendor that can transform the broken easterner such as Grey into the manly, awakened westerner.

Setting, as Grey acknowledged, cannot be the most important feature in fiction.[23] Setting can instill atmosphere but it cannot keep pages turning and sustain interest. When Grey subordinated setting to characterization and plot, he created truly memorable heroes and heroines, and hence, great novels. In *Last of the Plainsmen* Buffalo Jones emerges as the major character—but he must share the role with a wild mustang named White Streak.

Grey was smitten with the capricious horses of the Grand Canyon. They embodied some of the aspects that he loved about the West: reckless power, unchecked passion, sleek elegance, and the raw elemental core of being. He came to worship them. So great was their power over him that they reappear time after time in such novels as *Heritage of the Desert, Riders of the Purple Sage,* and *Wildfire.* Frequently, as with White Streak, they become super-horses, able to fly at breakneck speed and leap gaping chasms. At a point in the narrative of *Last of the Plainsmen,* when Jones is unable to capture White Streak, Grey trembles with joy.

If Grey praises the abilities of the wild horses, he does not have the same reverence for the mountain lions of the Grand Canyon. Their capture by Jones, Emmett, and others forms the highlight—or lowlight for modern readers—of Grey's remarkable trip into the northern desert. The action of the hunt, the effort to track and rope the mountain lion, is tainted for readers today by its lack of morality or concern for the animal's welfare. For readers in 1908, already enamored of the current exploits of Teddy Roosevelt in a whirlwind hunting trip through the West, it was manly sport. By that time the buffalo was nearly eradicated, the beaver had been hunted to near extinction, and what remained—the American lion—became the target of early-twentieth-century sportsmen.

Grey reveals that even though Buffalo Jones had turned conservationist he still maintained a casual disregard for the suffering of animals. Jim Emmett said of him that "he shore can make animals do what he wants. But I never seen a dog or horse that cared two bits for him."

Whether it is reverence for nature and animals or simply the thrill of the hunt, what leaps from the pages of *The Last of the Plainsmen* is Zane Grey's increasing attraction to the rough and tumble life. The endless vistas, the gritty dialogue of the men, the excitement of the trail, the danger that often clutched at his throat: from these features he assembled a body of knowledge and a storehouse of feelings that would stand him in good stead as a writer of western life.

Last of the Plainsmen ends with everyone hunched over the fire, reminiscing. Grey's first western work closes without too many disasters or spiritual discoveries. Its major achievement is that it supplies the foundation on which are built all of Grey's major novels.

In that respect, it was a bold beginning.

7 🐎

The Veteran Apprentice

The publication in 1908 of *The Last of the Plainsmen* was the turning point in Zane Grey's literary career. Ripley Hitchcock's observation that Grey could not write either "narrative or fiction" no doubt hurt him to the core, but it also galvanized something in the author. "He does not know," he repeated like a mantra. "*They* are all wrong."

Hitchcock's words *are* curious. Later he would apologize for them. He, of course, had rejected Grey's manuscripts before and perhaps he sensed that the aspiring author's work was still hopelessly immature. Roping and tracking lions in the Grand Canyon was adventurous stuff, but could modern adult audiences be attracted to it? The risk was too great. Hitchcock knew it; the other editors knew it. His remarks to Grey, however, besides being clearly untrue, were inappropriate.

Dolly rallied to support Grey, and he never forgot her constant vigil by his side. "Let no man ever doubt the faith and spirit and love of a woman."[1] Just after the book was published by Outing, Buffalo Jones traveled to New York and attended an autograph party in Grey's honor. He agreeably signed each book "the last of the Plainsmen." Grey remarked that Jones was "simply great that night, and the crowd went wild. When my book was delivered each table got up with a roar."[2] The party alleviated some of the painful feelings surrounding the book's rejection by several major publishers. And, too, Grey felt satisfaction now that Jones's exploits and experiments were finally being made public.

After Grey completed his book on Buffalo Jones, he did not begin a major project for a good while. Instead he wrote several lucrative magazine stories centered on adventure and fishing. Although the articles covered some of the bills, Grey and Dolly still depended on loans from Grey's brother R.C. "Cruising in Mexican Waters" appeared in *Field and Stream* in January 1908; "Lassoing Lions in the Siwash" was published in *Everybody's* in June; also in June "Tige's Lion," a dog story no doubt inspired by Jack London's *Call of the Wild,* appeared in *Field and Stream*. He had written for *Field and Stream* on a periodic basis since 1903, and clearly it had become a safe alternative to the upheavals of book publishing.

Five other successful articles, two of them in *Field and Stream,* would appear in 1909, during which he published a baseball book for boys—*The Short Stop*—and found a publisher for *The Last Trail*. The manuscript had been circulating among New York publishers for nearly three years before it was accepted by Outing, a decision that arose from their earlier publication of *The Last of the Plainsmen*.

When *The Last Trail* finally appeared, Grey was in the throes of writing his first major novel of the Southwest, a book whose themes, settings, and characters stemmed directly from his experiences in the Arizona Strip.

In April 1908 Zane Grey returned to northern Arizona and with Buffalo Jones, David Rust (a Mormon from southern Utah), Jim Owens (a ranger), and several other men scouted the area around Powell's Plateau. In a region known as Surprise Valley, watered by the

Thunder River, they discovered a lush oasis in the midst of the desert terrain. Grey was struck by the contradiction of vital life flourishing within the stark, hostile desert environment.

After leaving the valley they trekked northward to the villages of Fredonia, Arizona, and its sibling Kanab, Utah, both Mormon settlements. Mormon life attracted Grey: from Jim Emmett and his brood to the numerous others he had encountered in the high Southwestern desert he admired how they subsisted—indeed prevailed—like the tender shoots in Surprise Valley, while the land around simmered under the weight of the desert sun. For several days Grey talked with Mormon families in the two towns, mingling with the elders as well as the knots of children. He saw harmony amid the discord of life, and generous amounts of repression and domination.[3]

It was during this visit in April–May 1908 that Grey decided to incorporate the Mormon experience in northern Arizona and southern Utah into a western romance.[4] By that time he had met enough Mormons and absorbed enough of their customs and traditions to render them convincingly in fiction. He wandered through the settlements, observing the necessary fragments and wholes of the desert landscape in which to place his selected characters.

⚘

Grey was certainly not the first to scrutinize Mormon culture in the West. As early as the 1840s the melodramatic aspects of Mormonism were being explored, exploited, and sensationalized. In 1843 Frederick Marryat published *Monsieur Violet*, which took advantage of the public's limited knowledge of Mormon culture and inflated some of the more secretive features. Polygamy, of course, was central to the Mormon "menace" and writers from Bulwer-Lytton to Grey focused their energies on revealing some of its more suggestive and dangerous aspects. Bulwer-Lytton in his 1851 novel *Alice; or, the Mysteries* took a decidedly anti-polygamy stand, but his book tends to be more didactic fustian than serious fiction. Other anti-polygamy novels flourished in the 1850s and 1860s with titles as suggestive as those from any contemporary tattler: *The Prophets; or Mormonism Unveiled* (1855); *Female Life Among the Mormons* (1855); *Perversion; or the Causes and Consequences of Infidelity, a Tale of the Times* (1856); and *Mormon Wives* (1856).

By 1870 the most controversial features of Mormonism—polygamy, secret police, and golden plates—were showing up in articles and stories by both major and minor writers. Mark Twain and Artemus Ward joined the fray. More novels with Mormon subject matter appeared, among them Langdon E. Mitchell's *Two Mormons from Muddlety: Love in the Backwoods* (1876), and Charles Bertrand Lewis's *Bessie Bane; or, the Mormons' Victim* (1880). John Hansen Beadle's *Life in Utah; or, The Mysteries and Crimes of Mormonism* (1870), though anti-Mormon, was perhaps the most informed book of the lot. Beadle was editor of the *Salt Lake City Reporter* and hence was close to the activities and concerns of his Mormon friends and neighbors.

The melodramatic aspects of Mormonism stretched across the ocean to Europe. Arthur Conan Doyle in *A Study in Scarlet* related the story of how Jefferson Hope chased and killed two Mormons because they had murdered John Ferrier. Ferrier's daughter dies of a broken heart because of a forced marriage to one of the Mormons. Doyle later recanted his "rather sensational and over-coloured picture," but his novel endured as one of the most famous with Mormon subject matter.[5]

The pro-Mormon stance in literature emerged in 1898 with the publication of Nephi Anderson's *Added Upon,* which probed the beneficial qualities of Mormon culture and praised its liberating though restricted lifestyles. Harry Leon Wilson wrote of the spiritual struggle of Joel Rae in *Lions of the Lord* (1903), tracing his flight from persecution in Illinois to the Mountain Meadows Massacre in Utah.

In *Heritage of the Desert* (1910) Zane Grey was to continue and emphasize the pro-Mormon viewpoint, even though in later works he could take the opposite position. Grey's relationship with Emmett is largely responsible for his favorable views of Mormonism in *Heritage*;

Grey's investigation of the crueler aspects of it in the sprawling villages of Utah and Arizona prompted his disparaging perspectives in *Riders of the Purple Sage* (1912).

Zane Grey wrote the manuscript for *Heritage of the Desert* in longhand on the table at his Lackawaxen cottage. Working it over for grammar and punctuation, Dolly additionally made a second copy. She relished this aspect of her relationship with Grey because it afforded her a level of intimacy that Grey denied her in daily life. On paper she got to see her husband's heart and mind at work, his exuberances and moments of despair. She also recognized his emerging style and his increasing ability to edit tightly his own work.

When the two manuscripts were ready, Zane traveled to New York and delivered them personally: the first went to Harper's; the second to a minor publishing house, Street and Smith's. At Harper's Grey again stood before Ripley Hitchcock, placing the weighty manuscript on his desk. Grey looked him in the eye and said: "Mr. Hitchcock, I know you are convinced that I cannot write fiction, but this is the type of book I have always wanted to write.... I believe it is a good book.... I only ask as a personal favor that you read this manuscript yourself."[6]

Days later in Lackawaxen, Grey received a brief note from Hitchcock about discussing the manuscript. Grey left for New York, and by late morning was in the executive editor's office overlooking Franklin Square. Hitchcock beamed. More importantly, he shoved Harper's famous blue contract toward Grey for signature. Grey was so overcome with emotion that he could hardly render his name.

The Heritage of the Desert was published in the summer of 1910. The original dust jacket declared that it was "a rushing story of the Southwest ... full of action, in which men are swayed by primitive motives, facing death carelessly. Seldom has the 'elemental' note been sounded so truly."

Clearly it was the best book Zane Grey had yet written, a first-class romance with unusual maturity, poise, and beauty. The themes have not yet had a chance to descend into formula, and so the characters and settings have a surprising freshness and clarity.

The Heritage of the Desert can be quickly summarized thus: a wounded easterner (Jack Hare) is nursed back to health in the Utah desert by Mormon patriarch August Naab. Hare gradually learns the ways of sheep farming and the beliefs of the Mormon community. He soon falls in love with the half-Spaniard, half-Indian woman named Mescal, who by Mormon law is promised to Naab's son, Snap. To avoid marrying the drunken, lascivious Snap, Mescal flees into the desert. A year after her departure, Hare journeys into the desert to find her, eventually discovering her whereabouts in the Edenic canyon known as Thunder River. He brings Mescal back to civilization, and kills the notorious outlaw Holderness. After Snap Naab's death Hare marries Mescal in the Mormon community.

With the writing of *Heritage* Grey began a tradition of creating unusual character names. Examples are Hare (suggestive of "flight"), Naab (suggestive of capture), and Holderness (an arresting combination of "hold" and "wilderness"). Also, Holderness retains a foreman named Snood—which sounds curiously Dickensian. In other works leading characters are given four-letter first and last names, mirroring the form of Zane Grey. Even in *Heritage* peripheral characters such as Dene, Cole, and Snap Naab illustrate Grey's penchant for creating colorful, memorable short names.

Grey would go to great lengths to insure that his character names were descriptive and memorable. While researching the novel *Wyoming,* he had his son Romer drive him through rural parts of the Rockies. Grey sat on the passenger side and jotted down unusual names from the mailboxes they stopped at. Later at home Grey would mutter the names over and over, adjust letters and insert them on the page, waiting for just the right sound to ring true in his ear.

The first half of *Heritage of the Desert* deals with Jack Hare's recovery from his illness and with his introduction to the desert and Mormon culture. While regaining his strength in the care of Naab and his family,

Hare learned what conquering the desert made of a man. August Naab was close to threescore years; his chest was wide as a door, his

arm like the branch of an oak. He was a blacksmith, a mechanic, a car-
penter, a cooper, a potter. At his forge and in his shop, everywhere
were crude tools, wagons, farming implements, sets of buckskin har-
ness, odds and ends of nameless things, eloquent and pregnant proof
of the fact that necessity is the mother of invention. He was a mason;
the levee that buffeted back the rage of the Colorado in flood, the wall
that turned the creek, the irrigation tunnel, the zigzag trail cut on the
face of the cliff—all these attested his eye for line, his judgment of distance, his strength in toil. He was a farmer, a cattle-man, a grafter of
fruit-trees, a breeder of horses, a herder of sheep, a preacher, a physi-
cian. Best and strangest of all in this wonderful man was the instinct
and the heart to heal. "I don't combat the doctrine of the Mormon
church," he said, "but I administer a little medicine with my healing. I
learned that from the Navajos." The children ran to him with bruised
heads, and cut fingers, and stubbed toes; and his blacksmith's hands
were as gentle as a woman's. . . . The farm was overrun by Navajo
sheep which he had found strayed and lost on the desert. Anything
hurt or helpless had in August Naab a friend. Hare found himself
looking up to a great and luminous figure, and he loved this man.
(pp. 58–59)

The second half of *Heritage of the Desert* is a classic example of the
hero's journey from mythology.[7] Hare is, in fact, awakened to the
desert, but is as yet untested by it. The initial part of the book is Hare's
preparation for his rite of passage. Hence, his spiritual growth is limited until his flight to find Mescal during the second half of the book.
Only when he makes his arduous journey through the desert can Hare
reach manly stature.

On the first anniversary of Mescal's departure,[8] Hare is summoned
to the adventure that will allow him to know "the heritage of the
desert." Led by Mescal's dog Wolf, he enters the unknown desert and
begins to cross what Grey calls the "somber line." This somber line
marking the known from the unknown is also the passage into manhood that Hare both fears and desires. Another animal helper, the
super-horse Silvermane, aids Hare in his search for Mescal. Assisted
by his animal companions, Hare encounters the vastness, terror, and

delight of the sprawling desert, ultimately arriving in the Edenic setting of Thunder River Canyon—the literary equivalent of Dillon's Falls in Grey's boyhood Ohio.

Grey was always fascinated by a lush oasis in the midst of the desert. It represented for him a place of nourishment and refuge in the middle of chaos and evil. Grey called Dillon's Falls the "greatest place in the world."[9] It is no wonder that his idyllic childhood place would show up in Western guise in such books as *Heritage of the Desert* and *Riders of the Purple Sage.*

After his journey, Hare finds Mescal, "his desert flower." But to Hare she is more than simply that. She represents all the mysteries and secrets of the desert; she embodies the desert, the terrible and primitive unknown that excites Hare. When Mescal flees to the desert, a character says that "she has become one of the sands of the desert." She is the great "knower" of the wasteland. Hare is the one who seeks to know. By being near her, he partakes of her desert wisdom.

Hare, however, cannot stay in the paradise of Thunder River Canyon, as Odysseus cannot stay among the Lotus-Eaters. Grey's heroes are a restless bunch, always made nervous by joy and a woman's charms. Hare must return to the Mormon community. "'There's no place for us to go,'" Hare admits. "'We can't live the life of Indians.'" The return through more treacherous obstacles completes the journey's cycle of departure, initiation, and return. Already "psychically" married, Hare and Mescal along with Silvermane and Wolf come back to August Naab's settlement.

After two years in the wasteland and with his heroic journey completed, Hare comes to know the "heritage" surrounding him. His great psychological awareness comes with his marriage to Mescal, the knower and earth mother, who gives him the gift of insight and wisdom. In Mescal's eyes Hare sees "the dark gateways of the desert open only to him."[10] In the romantic tradition Hare's union with Mescal symbolizes his triumph over evil and his mastery of life—the necessary ingredients of wish-fulfillment.

Rider on the Wind

By 1911 Grey could boast of five novels (*Betty Zane, The Spirit of the Border, The Last Trail, The Last of the Plainsmen,* and *The Heritage of the Desert*), two books for young adults (*The Short Stop* and *The Young Forester*), and twenty-three articles for such diverse periodicals as *Field and Stream, Popular,* and *Success. Heritage of the Desert* was selling well—close to thirty thousand copies the first month of publication—and Grey turned his attention to a new project.

After his morning hike on the trails around Lackawaxen, he would return to the cottage and resume his stint on the treadmill of words that was becoming both exhilarating and exhausting. He was working on *Riders of the Purple Sage* and the manuscript pages were mounting. Grey threw himself furiously into the project, hoping to follow the success of *Heritage* with another book about the Southwest, his new-found literary venue. Dolly was distracted with the raising of young Romer Grey, now over a year old.

In *Riders of the Purple Sage* Grey naturally turned to the mesas, canyons, and people of northern Arizona and southern Utah. It was for him a sanctified place and it remained so all his life. He believed that the whites in the region, having learned "the heritage of the desert," personified the "highest evolutionary form of humanity."[1] Because the Indians shared this sacred territory they were in fact superior to whites who lived elsewhere. But since the Indians had lost the region through warfare, they were inferior to their victors: the Mormons scattered throughout the Arizona Strip. This was Grey's reasoning, which employed a simplistic but straightforward version of Darwinism.[2]

If *Heritage of the Desert* was generally pro-Mormon in characterization and outlook, *Riders* was just the opposite. Although Grey loved specific Mormons, he thought in general that they mistreated women and were fanatical in their beliefs.[3] In his new book Grey probed this extremism in Mormon culture and revealed the tragic results of its application.

For Harper and Brothers the anti-Mormon sentiment was excessive, and they declined to publish *Riders of the Purple Sage.* Ripley Hitchcock stood firm in his decision, agreeing with Grey that it was a better novel than *Heritage* but explaining to him that it showed intolerance of the Mormons' beliefs. Hitchcock did consent to a vote among Harper's editors before giving Grey a final decision. Again, rejection—even minor—hit Grey hard and he went back to Lackawaxen a bitter and angry man.

While Harper's editors deliberated about the fate of *Riders,* Grey returned to Arizona, to the very countryside he had written about so vividly in his major novels. As it turned out, Buffalo Jones was away on an African tour and Jim Emmett was unavailable. Moreover, David Dexter Rust, with whom Grey had traveled in 1907 and 1908, could not cross Lee's Ferry because of spring flooding of the Colorado River. Grey was forced to hire veteran guide Al Doyle, a shiftless sourdough who was at various times a freighter, cowboy, rancher, buffalo hunter, and tracklayer for the Union Pacific Railroad. Zane was fortunate to discover Doyle. Like Buffalo Jones, and Jim Emmett, Doyle combined a thorough knowledge of western lore with a vibrant personality. His tales both fired and soothed Grey, particularly at a time when the author was fretting about the fate of *Riders of the Purple Sage*.

Doyle and Grey headed northeast of Flagstaff toward Marsh Pass and the gigantic sprawl of the Navaho-Hopi reservation near the Four Corners. Grey witnessed again the startling palette of the Painted Desert with its ochres, lavenders, pale blues, and viridians. After traversing the pass, they came to the trading post at Kayenta, in the heart of Navaho country. The post was operated by John and Louisa Wetherill. The Wetherills had been at the reservation since 1906, and had continued a tradition of benevolence toward and a general concern for the Navaho people. Louisa Wetherill, in particular, inspired several Grey novels dealing with the reservation. No doubt it was Louisa who first told Grey of the problems on the reservation, problems and conflicts he was to analyze in *The Vanishing American* (1925). The same is true of the issues in *The Rainbow Trail*, which come directly from the Wetherills' trading post at Kayenta.[4]

The Wetherills appear in *The Rainbow Trail* with the name of Withers, and Grey remarks that Louisa "was held in peculiar reverence and affection by both tribes in that part of the country. Probably she knew more of the Indians' habits, religion, and life than any white person in the West."[5]

The visit to the reservation in 1911 was Grey's first extensive encounter with the culture of the American Indian. He had researched the histories of some of the eastern tribes for his Ohio River trilogy, but the western Native American remained largely a mystery to him. Representations of them he had seen through dime novel illustrations and those of Frederic Remington. Of course his head was filled with countless yarns concerning the Indians' "bloodlust," resourcefulness, and, yes—spirituality. The Indians' reputed violence, however, never impressed Grey. But their spirituality and their complete identification with nature won him over. It was this reverence for the Indian that prompted Grey to see their struggle in highly romanticized terms. In Kayenta he saw the squalid conditions and absorbed the Navaho's customs and culture on the reservation. He never, however, reached below the surface of Native American culture, preferring instead to create an idealized vision of the Indian, much like that of a majority of the writers and painters of the nineteenth century.

From his visit to Arizona he concluded that the Native American races were dying, an idea not totally supported by the census figures from that period.[6] But he clung to this belief and it became the theme of his major work of the twenties, *The Vanishing American.* At one point in this novel Grey remarks that "the Indian's deeds are done. His sun has set." This disparaging view may be due in part to his utter disbelief in the missionary system and the failure of education on the reservations. For Grey the entire attempt to force Anglo values on Indian children was a clear indication that the Indian would lose his identity, his own unique vision, and consequently, his heritage.[7] And because Grey was one-thirty-second Indian on his mother's side, he perhaps thought himself a brother in the Indian's struggle for recognition. More importantly, he thought he could become their voice.

This 1911 journey to the Navaho reservation fired something in Grey. He began to see the Indians' side of the struggle for territory and identity, a breakthrough which was to have serious and enduring ramifications in his work. Additionally, during Grey's and Doyle's sojourn with the Wetherills, the subject of the Rainbow Bridge in southern Utah came up. "Nonnezoshe" (Navaho for "a rainbow turned to stone") was the immense rock arch rearing 278 feet over the stony floor of the American outback, a monument sacred to the Navaho but so remote that few Anglos had seen it. John Wetherill had traveled to the site as a member of the first Anglo expedition, only two years earlier. Grey's interest was piqued. The bridge was over a hundred miles from the trading post at Kayenta, and the entire trek had to be made on horseback or on foot. Grey pressed Wetherill to try it, but the latter perhaps thought the trip too long and arduous for unseasoned travelers. Zane had to wait two more years before being able to witness the mystic strength of Nonnezoshe.

After continuing on to Mexico, Grey returned to Lackawaxen and to the news that *Riders of the Purple Sage* had been rejected by

Harper's. By the time he got off the train in New York, he had already made up his mind to go above Ripley Hitchcock and see the vice president of Harper and Brothers, Mr. Duneka. Duneka was aware that his editors had rejected *Riders* unanimously; however, Grey urged him to read it for himself. Duneka deliberated for a moment, considered the urgency in Grey's voice, and remarked that he would do just that. Grey reminded Duneka that *Heritage of the Desert* was successful and that Harper's had published three of his young adult books. Grey wanted to stay with Harper's. Duneka, more a diplomat than Hitchcock, said that he would give the manuscript his personal attention and have an answer for Grey shortly.[8]

Somewhat appeased, Grey returned to Lackawaxen on the afternoon train and began the agonizing wait for Duneka's decision. During these periods of inactivity, depression continued to stalk Grey. This chronic nemesis, combined with worries over his family's well-being, the dwindling royalty checks from *Heritage of the Desert,* the strain of *Riders'* tenuous status, and virtually anything outside of daily routine, continued to undermine Grey's health. Clearly, he had to write or he would have gone mad. He did some preparatory work on a young adult book, *Ken Ward in the Jungle,* which he had researched in Mexico only shortly before. Dolly was pregnant again and due to give birth in the spring of 1912.

Within a week he was back in Duneka's office. The vice president had read Grey's book—so had his wife—and both gave it fulsome praise. Duneka added that Harper's wanted to publish it; they would also give it a strong promotional campaign. Grey was speechless with pleasure.

Riders of the Purple Sage, the book that had such a jolting ride to publication, burst upon the literary scene in 1912—and was gobbled up. Its financial success, however, can be explained more easily than its literary merits. As for the latter, the book is difficult to analyze due to its numerous intricacies of plot, twists, ironies, inconsistencies, and mistaken identities. These features of course are the hallmarks of opera and romance, and Grey uses them deftly and plentifully.

Put simply, *Riders of the Purple Sage* is the story of two romantic relationships, one of which develops in a state of purity and innocence, while the other unfolds surrounded by turmoil and death. The first, the Venters-Bess relationship, is the more idyllic of the two, the one closer to ultimate wish-fulfillment. The Lassiter-Jane Withersteen relationship is complex, tangled, and curiously elusive to analyze.

Jane Withersteen has inherited the sprawling ranch named Cottonwoods in southern Utah, an area experiencing unaccustomed "unrest and strife" as the story begins.

> She owned all the ground and many of the cottages. Withersteen House was hers, and the great ranch, with its thousands of cattle, and the swiftest horses of the sage. To her belonged Amber Spring, the water which gave verdure and beauty to the village and made living possible on that wild purple upland waste. She could not escape being involved by whatever befell Cottonwoods.
>
> That year, 1871, had marked a change which had been gradually coming in the lives of the peace-loving Mormons of the border. Glaze—Stone Bridge—Sterling, villages to the north, had risen against the invasion of Gentile settlers and the forays of rustlers. There had been opposition to the one and fighting with the other. And now Cottonwoods had begun to wake and bestir itself and grow hard.

In the opening pages of the novel, Jane is awaiting the arrival of churchmen who increasingly resent her friendship with Gentiles. In her late twenties, she is "promised" in marriage to the shadowy Mormon elder by the name of Tull. One of her riders, Bern Venters, early in the novel is torn nearly to shreds by Tull and his henchmen. Venters is saved by the black-garbed, fearsome Jim Lassiter—a sort of Lew Wetzel in chaps, who hates Mormons and spends a good part of his time killing them.

After fleeing Cottonwoods Venters encounters a masked rider near Deception Pass in southern Utah. Venters shoots him—or her as it turns out. With a wounded Bess in tow, Venters seeks safety in a lush protected valley he calls Surprise Valley, an area left by the ancient cliff dwellers centuries before. Thus unfolds the development of Bess's and

Venters's relationship amid a Crusoe-like backdrop of indolent water-falls, pristine vistas, and abundant game. In many ways the valley takes on the look of a Garden of Eden, or more to the point, a primitive and nourishing Shangri-la in the heart of the desert and plateau country. As Bess recovers from her gunshot wound, she falls in love with Bern and he with her. In this state of uncorrupted innocence, they pursue their relationship much as the members of the Anasazi community did centuries earlier. Grey's point is that love between a man and a woman in a chaotic world is the highest form of fulfillment, and is metaphorically related to the verdant canyon in the middle of the bleakness and savagery of the surrounding desert.

Parallel with the Venters-Bess plot is the one of Lassiter and Withersteen, who until the end of the novel has managed to avoid Tull's advances. Central to the plot is the slow death of Cottonwoods. Threatened by rustlers and encroaching Mormons, Jane's estate becomes a backdrop of impending doom through most of the novel, thus setting up Lassiter's and Withersteen's passage into a new life at the end. Grey, however, imbues Jane Withersteen with excessive and gratuitous emotionalism. At one point she angrily retreats to her room and becomes a "sightless, voiceless . . . writhing living flame. And she tossed there while her fury burned and burned, and finally burned itself out." Like other Grey heroines, Jane Withersteen has a curious fascination for the guns of her male companions. Her feelings toward Lassiter's firearm are a mixture of both attraction and repulsion: "Jane slipped her hands down to the swinging gun sheaths, and when she locked her fingers around the huge, cold handles, she trembled as with a chilling ripple over all her body."

Beyond any sexual intent, Jane has the mind of a true reformer. "'May I take your guns?'" she asks Lassiter. "'Why?'" says Jim. "'It's no trifle,'" admits Jane, "'no woman's whim—it's deep—as my heart . . . I want to keep you from killing more men—more Mormons. You must let me save you from more wickedness . . . I feel that if I can't change you—then soon you'll go out to kill . . . Lassiter, if you care a little for me—let me—for my sake—let me take your guns!'"

Of course, most of Grey's characters live under the delusion that they can change other people. They manipulate, coerce, and in most cases devote much of their lives to trying to rescue other people—even if these "victims" don't welcome the efforts made on their behalf. Grey assumes that a woman's highest aspiration is to be swept away by a male dragon-slayer. In his Mormon novels, his female characters are set up to be the innocent victims of some Mormon's evil intent, while his male heroes roam the countryside, involving themselves in a fracas whenever some leering elder tries to subjugate a helpless heroine.

Jim Lassiter is the prototype of the six-gun hero in western romance fiction and film, a durable, laconic, footloose sort who is driven by hatred and vengeance but eventually hangs up his firearms for the love of a woman. Lassiter is an absolute meddler in other people's lives. When he tracks Venters to Surprise Valley he does it for the curious reason of making sure the canyon is "safe" for Venters to inhabit. After he meets and falls in love with Jane Withersteen, Jim Lassiter gives up self, preferring to perform tasks that please Jane solely. When he threatens to kill Bishop Dyer, he does it for Jane's sake, not for his own. Clearly, Lassiter's identity is tied to other people's lives, wishes, and whims.

As Jane's estate becomes too dangerous for her and Lassiter, they flee southward to join Bern Venters and Bess in the safety of Surprise Valley. They scale the hidden entrance to the valley, pursued by Tull and his men. A huge rock guards the passage. Lassiter dislodges the stone and sends it crashing down on their pursuers—on Tull in particular and Mormonism in general. Jane and Lassiter take up new lives in the valley with Bess and Venters. Ironically, through the whole novel Jane has been pleading with Lassiter to give up his guns, only to arrive in this peaceful canyon where no guns are necessary—at least, not for killing rustlers and Mormons. And so, Jane and Jim, like Bern and Bess before them, enter and subdue paradise, while the rest of the discordant world carries on around them. The book ends before the reader can see what happens to their relationship, but can nonetheless be fairly certain that it proceeds much like that of Bern and Bess.

Whatever one might think of Grey's incredible plot, the title is nothing short of masterful. *Riders of the Purple Sage* is probably the most colorful—and generic—of the early Grey titles. Specifically, "riders" usually connotes something masculine and delightfully sinister. Used in combination with the sensory words "purple sage," it captures the mystery, romance, and spacious landscape of the American southwest.

Despite its defects as a novel, *Riders of the Purple Sage* defined the genre for the western romance. For 1912 audiences, accustomed to the manly exploits of Teddy Roosevelt, the book assured them that the Wild West was still alive and that it was still filled with resourceful heroes, swooning women, rowdy cowboys, and a clear if violent moral code. Additionally, this audience included a host of new immigrants to America's shores. Between 1900 and 1912 many Italians, Slavs, and Britons entered the United States, eager to read about its heritage, and Grey's brand of western romance provided a straightforward, if skewed, perspective on life west of the Mississippi. All of these ingredients—Grey's intricate, romantic tale, an increased awareness of the West through the adventures of Teddy Roosevelt, and an enlarged audience—combined to ensure *Riders* instant and later enduring success.

To the Desert Born

Zane Grey turned forty in early 1912, the year his most famous and perhaps most accomplished novel was published.

In February of that year, as Lackawaxen lay robed in snow, Grey was again heading to Arizona, to a West that was undergoing drastic changes amid the more permanent landscape features. New Mexico and Arizona, for instance, once notoriously lawless territories, were entering the Union as states. Emigration to the West was increasing yearly, and Hollywood had recently become the center of the motion picture industry. Rail lines linking the east to the west were being completed. Veterans like the sixty-five-year-old artist Thomas Moran returned to the Grand Canyon to scout suitable epic locations for paintings. And struggling apprentices like Zane Grey were exploring Arizona's deserts hoping to make a mark of their own. The Old West was fading, but one author seemed bent on perpetuating its romantic, halcyon days.

Grey headed to southern Arizona on a suggestion by Robert Hobart Davis, editor of *Munsey's Magazine*. Zane was in search of new material and Davis offered him the idea of researching the tensions along the U.S.–Mexican border.[1]

Arriving in the desert near Tucson, Grey witnessed the full extent of revolutionary fervor there. The revolution to overthrow the Diaz government in Mexico had been in motion since 1910. The leader of the opposition, Francisco Madero, with supporters Pancho Villa and Emiliano Zapata, frequently raided the small settlements in northern Mexico and the southern U.S. By the time of Grey's arrival and because of Arizona's impending statehood, eighty thousand American troops were stationed along the volatile border to protect residents. However, holes in the American bulwark were many. Mexican revolutionaries found weaknesses in the American line, plundering the ranches and farms just across the border. They terrorized Americans and stole their livestock and food, killing any resisting ranchers or herders. From these outrages Grey developed a fierce hatred of the Mexican guerrillas, and later, of Mexicans in general.[2]

Adding fuel to this bias was the Mexican government's treatment of the Yaqui Indians in Sonora.[3] The brutal Mexican regime began exploiting the Yaquis in the late 1800s and the Indians withdrew to the mountains to resist their oppressors. After starving out the Yaquis, the Mexicans sold them into slavery and forced them to work on the hemp plantations on the Yucatan Peninsula. Very few Yaquis returned to Sonora, but those who did never forgot their struggle for freedom and dignity.

Grey sympathized with the Yaquis, in particular because he believed that they descended from the Aztecs.[4] In turn he blamed the Mexicans for their abuse and victimization. From this perspective of the Mexican character he developed some conflicting views. On one hand he could see them as devious and cruel, and on the other as arrogant and lazy. He praised the "true Spanish" of Spain who had no Indian blood, but he remarked that the Mexicans were "subtle and mysterious. . . . They work in secret, in the dark. They are dominated first by religion, then by gold, then by the passion for a woman . . ."[5] Grey's stereotyping of Mexicans becomes evident in his next two books, *Desert Gold* (1913) and *The Light of Western Stars* (1914).

Grey cavorting with bears near the Mogollon Rim, Arizona, c. 1920. *Courtesy of the G. M. Farley Collection, Hagerstown, Maryland*

The switching of venues from northern to southern Arizona allowed Grey a different look at the desert with which he was presently smitten. Saguaro cactus, vast stretches of sand, and yucca replaced the towering rock fingers and pine-spangled canyons of the northern mountains. Here in this blistering, vacant world only the most hardy persevered, prompting Grey to observe that the desert magnified both evil and good qualities of character.

Desert Gold focuses on the seething Mexican border in 1912–13 and the sere desert landscape around Tucson. Clearly inferior as a novel to both *Heritage of the Desert* and *Riders of the Purple Sage*, the book has for its main character Dick Gale, who embodies the traits of many of Zane Grey's protagonists: a well-meaning but confused easterner who comes to receive the "education" of the West. The land too adds to his transformation by first tempering character and later molding it into heroic proportions. This reliance on nature as the ultimate moral guide comes directly from Wordsworth: "one impulse from a vernal wood / may teach you more of man / of moral evil and of good / than all the sages can."

A college football player, Gale argues with his father and heads west to find his fortune. Predictably, he becomes embroiled in the revolutionary events along the border. *Desert Gold* differs from Grey's two previous novels in that it is set in the present, a rather strategic move on the author's part because it beckons to the reader—he or she, too, can be part of the current western experience. This superficial romance of the border, however, quickly slips into slick melodrama, as coincidences complicate an already strained plot. What saves the novel are Grey's passionate and sometimes penetrating observations of the southern desert:

> They had scarcely covered a mile when a desert-wide, moaning, yellow wall of flying sand swooped down upon them. . . . The moan increased to a roar, and the dull red slowly dimmed, to disappear in the yellow pall, and the air grew thick and dark. . . .
>
> . . . The steady, hollow bellow of flying sand went on. It flew so thickly that enough sifted down under the shelving rock to weight the blankets and almost bury the men. They were frequently compelled to shake off the sand to keep from being borne to the ground. . . . The floor of their shelter gradually rose higher and higher. They tried to eat, and seemed to be grinding only sand between their teeth. . . . They could only crouch close to the leaning rock, shake off the sand, blindly dig out their packs, and every moment gasp and cough and choke to fight suffocation.
>
> The storm finally blew itself out. . . . Far as eye could reach the desert had marvelously changed; it was now a rippling sea of sand dunes. (p. 16)

Indeed, if it were not for Grey's knowledge of atmospheric effects and landscape feature details his books would bog down swiftly. It is generally the land that saves a poorly conceived character or an ill-drawn situation.

Desert Gold appeared in 1913, and like the previous Grey novels was illustrated both on the dust cover and throughout the text. Without a doubt the host of Zane Grey illustrators made a substantial contribution to his success and helped to bring to life a score of characters for a wide, receptive audience.

Some of the best illustrators in the world were working in New York publishing houses during the years 1910 to 1920. *Popular* magazine, which serialized *Heritage of the Desert* in 1910, had a coterie of superb artists, many of whom had studied under the fabled Howard Pyle. During this period, *Popular*'s semi-monthly circulation topped three hundred thousand copies. It was an imitation of *Argosy* magazine, featuring fiction exclusively. *Popular*'s artists included Douglas Duer (now famous for illustrating the original *Riders of the Purple Sage*), Frank Schoonover, N. C. Wyeth, Charlie Russell, Herbert W. "Buck" Dunton, Oliver Kemp, Harold Brett, and W. H. D. Koerner. Although they actually freelanced for other periodicals and book publishers, *Popular*'s editors claimed them as their own for publicity purposes.

Douglas Duer, who would go on to illustrate several Grey titles, was a student of Howard Pyle and a neophyte in matters concerning the West. However, he diligently researched his subjects and created a body of work more noted for technique than originality. His illustrations for *Riders,* though technically accomplished, are unconvincing regarding the landscape of southern Utah.

N. C. Wyeth, perhaps the most famous of Pyle's pupils, was in high demand for both books and magazines. Wyeth's ascent paralleled Grey's rise to success, and by 1915, with his numerous book illustration contracts, he was arguably the most respected, well-paid, and recognized commercial artist in the world. But even though Wyeth admired Zane Grey's work, he confessed in 1910 that his "ardor for the West [was] slowly . . . dwindling, until my desires to go there to paint its people are already lukewarm."[6]

When Frederic Remington died in 1909, a legacy vanished with him. Praised as the West's most important visual artist, Remington almost single-handedly brought the West to eastern audiences through his numerous illustrations and paintings. Nearly equal to Remington in stature was Charlie Russell, who continued the tradition but took his own tack in western illustration. What Duer lacked in western knowledge, Russell possessed in abundance. Russell worked for *Popular* while he was amassing a body of painting and sculpture notable for its accuracy, imagination, and vigor. Like Remington, Russell built a reputation both as an illustrator and as a fine artist. Rumpled and flinty-looking, with a kind of rawhide, folksy sincerity, Russell epitomized the rugged and independent spirit of the West.

"Buck" Dunton was an easterner by birth and a westerner by predilection. Born in Maine, he spent his early life tramping western trails, taming broncos, and roping cattle from the Canadian border to Mexico. His knowledge of western culture and lore was extensive and this translated into imaginative designs marked by excellent drawing and vivid color. Although Dunton worked in New York City, his heart was always roaming in the West. Nineteen twelve, the year of New Mexico's statehood, found him in Taos. He had discovered the town's light and landforms, and hoped to join fellow illustrator Ernest Blumenschein in spending his summers there. Eventually the art colony blossomed into the famous Taos Society of Artists, Dunton being one of the six original members.[7] Blumenschein once observed that illustrating Jack London's novels "made him and me." For Dunton, being a Zane Grey illustrator ensured the success of his career. Dunton retired from illustrating in 1924, devoting the rest of his life to capturing Taos and environs. At his easel he liked to wear a colorful bandanna and a large Stetson. With his hat tilted rakishly over one eye, and sporting a rather generous mustache, he looked straight out of the pages of a Grey novel.

One of Zane Grey's favorite illustrators was W. H. D. Koerner, who combined exceptional drawing skills with loose, daring brushwork and a talent for creating dramatic compositions. A student of Howard Pyle and later a pupil at the Art Students' League, Koerner at various times illustrated for the *Saturday Evening Post* and *Cosmopolitan* in addition to *Popular*. He also had a close association with Grey's publisher, Harper and Brothers, who produced *Harper's Weekly* and *Harper's Monthly*. It was a policy of the editors of *Harper's Monthly* not to use an artist more than once in a single issue. However, Koerner's talents were such that the editors allowed his work to appear twice or three times in an issue.[8]

One of Koerner's first Grey commissions was for *Country Gentleman,* which serialized *Desert of Wheat* (1919). Koerner drew eleven illustrations for the serial and later was approached by the same magazine to illustrate another Grey romance, *The Mysterious Rider.* Koerner was fully booked at the time and the editors turned to Frank B. Hoffman, an artist a whole cut below Koerner in talent. Hoffman's sketches came out as superficial and conventional, lacking the gusto and imagination that Koerner could have given the images.[9]

Grey was particularly attracted to the sixteen illustrations Koerner did for *Sunset Pass* (1931), and the pen and ink drawings for *Drift Fence* (1935). Grey's admiration for Koerner's work is evidenced by the letter Thomas B. Stanley (*American* magazine art editor) sent to Koerner in February 1928: "Zane Grey was in the office yesterday and was greatly pleased with your illustrations for Sunset Pass. . . . We were telling him how much we like them . . . and he said, 'You don't need to tell me; I know good pictures when I see them.' I know that you said that the waiting line was already formed for that picture, but I said I would write you and see what could be done. . . . tell us when you come up [to New York] next time."[10]

An illustrator outside the *Popular* circle was Frank Tenney Johnson, whose illustrations for Grey's *Lone Star Ranger* (1915) are notable for their authenticity and style. Johnson's knowledge of the West ran deep, and in the tradition of Remington, Russell, Dunton, and Harold von Schmidt, he capitalized on it in both book and magazine publishing. He was also famous for the Western scenes on calendars from Brown and Bigelow of Minneapolis. Additionally, he created a reputation outside illustration through several important paintings with western themes and settings.

Most of these painters, especially Dunton and Duer, advanced their careers through contact with the Zane Grey mystique. Moreover, their vivid illustrations helped strengthen and solidify that mystique in the eyes of a whole generation of readers worldwide.

10

The Awful, Windy Emptiness

Zane Grey made two major trips during the first half of 1913, one west and the other to Long Key, Florida. Elizabeth Zane Grey was nearly a year old and *Desert Gold* was appearing in serialization in *Popular* beginning in March. Harper and Brothers published it in book form directly after its serial run. *Riders of the Purple Sage* had netted fifty thousand dollars the previous year and similar success was predicted for *Desert Gold*.[1] It was safe to say that by early 1913 Grey had arrived as an established, successful author. Fame awaited. It was also safe to admit that Grey had discovered the formulaic western romance. With *The Heritage of the Desert* he glimpsed its possibilities; with *Riders of the Purple Sage* he was basically secure with it; but with *Desert Gold* and the beginning of his next book, *The Light of Western Stars,* the confirmation hit him like a lightning bolt. All other considerations for fiction (except those involving baseball and fishing) were shoved aside. Grey would write about the West with few exceptions.

As predictable as the robin's song was Grey's annual flight from

Lackawaxen. He was at Long Key by March, thus establishing that resort as one of his favorites. *Desert Gold* was running in *Popular,* and a few of Grey's fishing buddies were kidding him about his new-found success. These friends were special to Grey. Some of them traveled all over the world with him later on, and most were near him when his more sophisticated acquaintances began to grate on his nerves. He trusted these venerable salts, much as he confided in brother R.C. and of course Dolly.

At Long Key Grey was seeking a more profound angling experience. Close to thirty years before in Zanesville, Old Muddy Miser had remarked to Grey that he would "go far afield" to catch the giant fish of the seven seas. "You must make fishing a labor of love," Old Miser added. And by March 1913, at forty-one years of age, Grey was near to fulfilling this prophesy by becoming one of the most knowledgeable and dedicated anglers in the country.

Grey started his career as a fresh-water fisherman in the waters near Zanesville and later in the Lackawaxen and Delaware Rivers. R.C. was a constant companion in those days—and continued to be now. The Delaware was one of Grey's favorite fishing rivers, and he knew its bends and shallows like a native. "Every fishing water has its secrets," Grey wrote of the river, but he knew that fresh-water fishing could never satisfy the adventure he craved. He loved the fighting quality of black bass and the serenity of inland waters, but the open sea continually lured him.

As his success grew Grey turned more and more to salt-water fishing. At Tampico in Mexico he fished for tarpon, or at Avalon on Catalina Island he caught tuna, one weighing 119 pounds. Later he reeled in a 316-pound striped marlin off Catalina and set a world record by landing a 758-pound blue fin tuna in Nova Scotia. Grey went on to become president of the Long Key Fishing Camp and also vice president of the Catalina Tuna Club.

Grey's commitment to fishing—and writing about it—was deep and lifelong. Indeed, his love of ocean and river rivaled his affection for the desert, and perhaps it is difficult to determine at various points in his

Grey examining a shark's jaw, New Zealand, c. 1931. Grey was an amateur zoologist and admirer of Charles Darwin. *Courtesy of the G. M. Farley Collection, Hagerstown, Maryland*

life which one claimed his soul. He noted in his diary that "the sea, from which all life springs, has been equally with the desert my teacher and religion." Perhaps, but it is noteworthy that Grey failed to produce a single good novel about the sea.

When fishing, Grey was highly competitive but was hardly ever satisfied with his accomplishments. Much of life for him was vacillation between one activity and other, always in search of the unattainable. If he heard that one of his fishing records had been broken, he would become overzealous to set a greater one.[2] Fishing, like writing, increasingly became part of an addictive cycle in which Grey could immerse himself and avoid the depressed moods that constantly attacked him.

The huge vastness of the open sea thrilled, vexed, and saddened Grey. During the long fishing voyages he frequently reflected on his own mortality: "The lure of the sea is some strange magic that makes men love what they fear. The solitude of the desert is more intimate than that of the sea. Death on the shifting barren sands seems less insupportable to the imagination that death out on the boundless ocean, in the awful, windy emptiness. Man's bones yearn for dust."[3]

At Long Key Grey worked in the mornings on his new novel, *The Light of Western Stars,* then spent the rest of the day fishing and trolling in the Gulf Stream. It was to be his first novel of New Mexico, which he had researched mostly on his border journey to Arizona the year before. Grey's knowledge of New Mexico was limited at this stage in his career, so much of the novel lacks a pronounced New Mexican flavor.

As was his custom, he worked quickly on the novel drafts. The plot tumbled out; the pencil raced across the page, scratching out entire lines, inserting new ones in the cramped space of the margin. Frequently he wrote the whole page over again, and then went on to the next, always anticipating the next plot turn or character introduction.

He wrote letters to Dolly in the evening, letters in which his guilt surfaces over temporarily abandoning her. His depressions, however, were few. The heavy writing schedule in the morning and the long hours spent in the sun and spray in the afternoons and early evenings consumed his thoughts and feelings. He wrote Dolly in late March asking if she would mind if he visited Arizona before coming home.[4] Dolly wrote back to tell him that she would be disappointed if he didn't.

Zane Grey on a fishing expedition in the South Pacific in the early 1930s. He remained both a deep-sea and fresh-water fisherman all his life, often seeking challenges in remote parts of the world. *Courtesy of the G. M. Farley Collection, Hagerstown, Maryland*

In between trips he had finished *The Light of Western Stars* and sent it to *Munsey's* magazine, which began serializing it in May 1913. The days of having to wait on some editor's decision were over. Harper and Brothers was his committed book publisher; magazines vied for serial rights.

Unlike *Heritage* and *Riders*, *The Light of Western Stars* does not open in the middle of the action. We are introduced to the heroine as she arrives at a train station in southern New Mexico.

> Madeline Hammond stood tapping a shapely foot on the floor, and with some amusement contrasted her reception in El Cajon with what it was when she left a train at the Grand Central. The only time she could remember ever having been alone like this was once when she had missed her maid and her train at a place outside of Versailles—an adventure that had been a novel and delightful break in the prescribed routine of her much-chaperoned life. She crossed the waiting-room to a window and, holding aside her veil, looked out. At first she could descry only a few dim lights, and these blurred in her sight. As her eyes grew accustomed to the darkness she saw a superbly built horse standing near the window. Beyond was a bare square. Or, if it was a street, it was the widest one Madeline had ever seen. The dim lights shone from low, flat buildings. She made out the dark shapes of many horses, all standing motionless with drooping heads. Through a hole in the window-glass came a cool breeze, and on it breathed a sound that struck coarsely upon her ear—a discordant mingling of laughter and shout, and the tramp of boots to the hard music of a phonograph.
>
> "Western revelry," mused Miss Hammond, as she left the window. "Now, what to do? I'll wait here. Perhaps the station agent will return soon, or Alfred will come for me."
>
> As she sat down to wait she reviewed the causes which accounted for the remarkable situation in which she found herself. That Madeline Hammond should be alone, at a late hour, in a dingy little Western railroad station, was indeed extraordinary. (pp. 2–3)

A wealthy, much-traveled, but disillusioned easterner, Madeline has come west to discover meaning in her life (by now the pattern is well entrenched). The exposition is beautifully handled by Grey—patient, insightful, poised—so that Madeline's motivations for seeking out the West are deftly explained. She may be Grey's finest characterization up till 1914. Complex and dignified but with a certain coltish grace, Madeline, or "Majesty," as she is called, fills the novel with credibility and charm.

The Light of Western Stars has neither the emotional excesses of *Riders of the Purple Sage* nor the spare nobility of *Heritage of the Desert.* Its great quality is the handling of character and situation. Here Madeline shines with exquisite clarity, much like the "light of western stars" that pulse over her New Mexican domain.

Madeline eventually creates an opulent country club in the middle of the desert, known as Her Majesty's Rancho. Eastern friends descend on the place, ready to spin their elaborate webs and to play golf on the crude but extensive links. As the novel progresses, the reader becomes quite aware of Majesty's growing attachment to the West and the separation from her former friends. She falls prey to "the light of western stars." She thinks innocently of returning to Newport and New York, but she can't. The East is corrupt, effeminate, and makes people self-indulgent and lazy. The West, however, builds men out of selfish, weak people—even ones like Madeline. She ends up having a male consciousness by taking on the activities and wearing the clothes of men. She is no longer content merely to be. The West makes her a doer.

She marries the inebriated but good-hearted cowboy, Gene Stewart (actually, as the reader discovers, she has been married to him, unbeknownst, since the beginning of the book). Madeline is Grey's first female protagonist since *Betty Zane* (1903), and like Betty, she rises to moments of personal bravery. After all, she has been readied in her resolve by encountering and enduring the crucible of the frontier. On a wild ride across the Mexican border, Majesty tries to find Gene Stewart, who has been captured by Mexican revolutionaries. Grey reverses the role of the male rescuer as Madeline feverishly searches for her "man" in the arid wilds. Her hunt becomes more fervent than those of most male characters created by Grey, as if the author were asserting that women's wills were more intense and passionate.

At one point, Madeline has difficulty believing that she has fallen for a cowboy. In Grey's West, however, equality reigns supreme. No kings, queens, princes, or potentates. All men and women are leveled by the sun, sand, and ache of time. Indeed, the closer one is to the land, in Grey's eyes, the more one is morally pure and capable of a relationship with anyone on earth. Grey writes:

> The cowboys all had secrets. Madeline learned some of them. She marveled most at the strange way in which they hid emotions, except of violence of mirth and temper so easily aroused. . . . Madeline had to believe that a hard and perilous life in a barren and wild country developed great principles in men. Living close to earth, under the cold, bleak peaks, on the dust-veiled desert, men grew like the nature that developed them—hard, fierce, terrible, perhaps, but big—big with elemental force.[5]

Of course these were the survival qualities that Grey incorporated into his personal life. They may have worked for his desert heroes, but they were hardly suited to a twentieth-century family man. The more he approached this myth of the durable cowboy, the more he became divorced from his friends, family, wife, and himself.

Although *The Light of Western Stars* has none of the mythical qualities of *Heritage of the Desert* and *Riders of the Purple Sage,* it has instead a credible, realistic unfolding of events. The colorful escapades along the U.S.-Mexican border circa 1911–1912 are deftly woven into the backdrop. Grey handles contemporary events with the precision that he paints historical ones. Nuance and shadings of character, somehow absent in *Riders,* surface in the person of Madeline and her circle of acquaintances. Grey never lets her character descend into a sniveling martyr like Jane Withersteen or a clinging vine like Bess Erne.

More a character study than an action novel, and more of a romp than a "thinking" novel, *The Light of Western Stars* is the anomaly in Zane Grey's early fiction and a provocative byway in an otherwise predictable trail.

After departing Long Key, Grey headed straight for the Arizona desert and arrived there in April 1913. From Flagstaff he rode northeast toward the Kayenta trading post, meeting guide Al Doyle, cook George Morgan, a Mormon cowboy named Joe Lee, and two women from New York, Lillian Wilhelm and Elma Swartz.[6] Lillian was Dolly's cousin and an aspiring artist hoping to illustrate one of Grey's books.[7]

The Wetherills were pleased to see Grey, who felt that here he was in one of the great places on earth. After a brief rest, the entourage, headed by Wetherill and the Paiute Indian guide, Nasja Begay, ventured north into the desert in search of the Rainbow Bridge. It was Nasja Begay who had first led John Wetherill to Nonnezoshe years earlier, so his knowledge of the northern Arizona–southern Utah border was extensive. On horseback the group picked their way through the sand, leading Wetherill's pack mules and a supply wagon.

They at first took a zigzag course, veering northeast to the Navaho ruins at Keet Seel, some sixty miles from the border and another hundred or so miles from the bridge itself. Grey reflected on "the silent, little stone houses with their vacant black-eye windows."[8] After departing the ruins, they headed into Monument Valley where Grey was awed by the towering pillars of sandstone, some rising like mighty castles against the sky and some tickling the clouds like gaunt fingers.

In 1913 Monument Valley and environs were still largely unexplored by whites, so for most of the party, including Grey, the landscape took on the character of some foreign country in a time long ago. From their camp below Navajo Mountain, they could see a long way across southern Utah, beyond the "yellow and purple corrugated world of distance."[9] Wetherill pointed out various spots on the horizon to Grey, including the Grand Canyon of the Colorado and Escalente Canyon.

As they guided their horses and pack mules to the northwest, Grey felt the weight of time and distance: "Sound, movement, and life seemed to have no fitness here. Ruin was there and desolation and decay. The meaning of the ages was flung at me. A man became nothing."[10] Days later they entered the rugged, wind-sculpted canyon containing the Rainbow Bridge. Huge, ponderous stone walls loomed over them as they walked their animals over the broken rock shards on the floor. They came around a canyon rim and in the distance, spanning the chasm, was the muscular, graceful stone arch, stained by the sunset's fading light.

"Nonnezoshe," muttered John Wetherill.

Grey stopped in his tracks, mesmerized. He remarked that "it absolutely silenced me. . . . I had a strange mystic perception that this rosy-hued, tremendous arch of stone was a goal I had failed to reach in some former life, but now had found."[11]

That night they camped under the bridge. Nasja Begay said a prayer to the stone god but refused to pass under it. Grey, however, wished to see it from several angles, and so he walked back and forth under it. He stared at its moon-gilded edges. The wind moaned softly and an owl hooted: "an echo of night, silence, gloom, melancholy, death, age, eternity," swept down the canyon.[12] Grey dozed off, but awoke to see the dark shadow slipping from the bridge and later to witness the sun creeping over its chipped edges, gradually transforming the shape "until once more the arch was a rainbow."

Zane took comfort in the idea that because of the arch's remote location the "tourist, the leisurely traveler, the comfort-loving motorist would never behold it: only by toil, sweat, endurance, and pain could any man ever look at Nonnezoshe."[13] Of course this is precisely how Grey's characters achieve wisdom and nobility, but his view that the bridge was too remote for the leisure traveler proved to be a bit of wishful thinking.

The Rainbow Bridge transfixed Zane Grey throughout his life. It became the masculine symbol—solid, heavy, heroic, eternal—of the American West, as the Grand Canyon became the female symbol.

This 1913 journey to witness the sands and monuments of northern Arizona and southern Utah, to seek out and behold Nonnezoshe, was arguably the most significant trek of Grey's life. There were the earlier travels to the Grand Canyon, the Arizona Strip with Buffalo Jones and Jim Emmett, the Kayenta trading post, the Coconino Plateau and Lee's Ferry, and later in life there would be thrilling adventures throughout the world. However, this singular trek into the desert inspired more good fiction and carried with it not only a journey into the unexplored heart of the American West, but an excursion into the depths of Grey's soul.

Moreover, Grey added to his knowledge of the miserable conditions existing on the Navaho reservation. He was, however, in no way capable, either emotionally or intellectually, of rendering the Navaho's struggle in large-scale fiction. That process would take the next ten years and some severe changes in his life to reach fruition. He did recognize the Navaho's victimization, and this is what initially moved him. Hence, Native Americans play an important but secondary role in the novels of 1909 to 1919, and into the early 1920s.

Grey returned to Lackawaxen in late spring, sufficiently moved and educated to begin work on his great novel featuring the bridge, *The Rainbow Trail*. The Wetherills figured prominently in the story, as did the reliable Paiute, Nasja Begay.

He was also working on a novel of Texas, titled *The Lone Star Ranger* (serialized in May 1914; published by Harper's in 1915), which told the story of the organization of the Texas Rangers in 1875.

Although *The Lone Star Ranger* was a major seller in 1915, *The Rainbow Trail* was a better novel that revealed Grey's acute understanding of the Arizona-Utah landscape and his growing awareness of the dangers of the missionary system on the Navaho reservations there.

11

Mister Zane Grey

Although Grey touted *The Rainbow Trail* as an "independent" novel, it is really the sequel to *Riders of the Purple Sage*. Set in the 1880s, *The Rainbow Trail* tells of how defrocked minister John Shefford comes West and attempts to determine the whereabouts of young Fay Larkin (of *Riders of the Purple Sage*). As a friend of Bern Venters in Illinois, Shefford hears of Surprise Valley and the unfolding of events with the Mormons in southern Utah. With his life in shambles, Shefford heads West hoping to tie up the loose ends of the Lassiter-Withersteen-Fay Larkin mystery. Like *The Heritage of the Desert*, *The Rainbow Trail* is a quest novel, and like most quest novels it works on different levels: Shefford's search for Jim Lassiter, Jane, and Fay; his arduous journey to find the Rainbow Bridge; but above all, it is his search for something to replace his lost spirituality. "Take away a man's religion," Robert Ruark once observed, "and you'd better replace it with something of value." For Shefford, the "something of value" becomes a quest fraught with danger and intrigue, and continues in his walk through the purgatory of the arid and open spaces.

The novel opens with a familiar Grey device. The character looks (either expectantly or with some hesitation) at the landscape he is about to walk into. The initial atmosphere is generated by the emotions felt by this character, be they fear, wonder, joy, etc. Most often it is a state of bewilderment and awe, as the character views the vast, vacant ridges and canyons ahead of him. And because Grey's characters stumble into the West facing a spiritual void, the landscape appears both repellent and attractive at the same time, creating the fierce push-pull of the opening pages.

Beginning his search in the Arizona desert, Shefford meets the trader, Presbrey (here Grey seems to be using a convolution of Presbyterian, since the conversation opens with Shefford's admission of shedding his religion). "'I was a minister of the Gospel,'" confesses Shefford; "'I've broken out—beyond all bounds. I want to see some wild life.'"

However, the motivation for Shefford's quest appears somewhat skewed. Apparently, Venters instills in him an overwhelming urgency to free Fay Larkin from Surprise Valley. That may be Venters's desire, but why does Shefford so willingly take up the cause? Fay Larkin, Lassiter, and Jane Withersteen are not family, nor even acquaintances. Why is Shefford prepared to risk life and limb on something Venters should be resolving for himself? Moreover, how can Venters or Shefford be assured that Fay Larkin, Lassiter, and Jane aren't happy as punch in Surprise Valley, and don't need some meddling, confused wanderer to interrupt their happy existence? The romantic always assumes that he or she knows what's good for other people, and so there is nearly always an underlying neurosis in the motivation.

Shefford devotes his life to rescuing people. He first rescues young Fay Larkin from the Mormons who wish to make her a sealed wife. Grey treats these Mormons as truly evil, suspicious, and possessive creatures. Shefford then sets off to rescue Lassiter and Withersteen from their idyllic life in Surprise Valley, never stopping to ask whether his actions are for his benefit or theirs.

He eventually discovers Lassiter and Jane Withersteen in the lush valley. Here a major inconsistency occurs in the text. In *Riders of the Purple Sage* Lassiter is around forty years of age. Twelve years have elapsed between the time that Lassiter rolled the stone to seal the valley and Shefford's arrival to rescue them. In this time Lassiter has curiously become an old man, complete with long white hair and lined face. Grey refers to him as "the old gunman," and Lassiter is reduced to a pathetic character who mumbles several trite cliché phrases. At fifty-two (or eighty as Grey would have us believe) Lassiter seems ancient in *The Rainbow Trail,* a gaunt, haggard shell of his former self.

What rings true, however, is the harrowing ride the group endures down the raging Colorado River, which serves as the climax of the novel. Shefford, Fay Larkin, Lassiter, Jane Withersteen, the Mormon boatman Joe Lake, and the guide Nas Ta Bega take the ride of their lives. Surrounded by the tall canyon walls and the fleeting, hectic colors, they plunge southward toward and through the Grand Canyon. Grey's description of the setting, actions, and emotions is some of the best writing in the novel, and genuinely reflects his ability to observe and record the impressions around him.

Just prior to the Colorado River sequence, Shefford and his comrades stumble upon the Rainbow Bridge. These encounters between character and unique landform often provoke Grey into excess emotionalism. However, when Shefford views the sweeping stone bridge, he experiences restrained, even mute, emotion. Looking for a rainbow in the West, he realizes that the natural arch is both his good luck piece and the bridge to his new-found spirituality.

With Fay Larkin, Jim Lassiter, and Jane Withersteen safe, with his completion of the desert ordeal and his pilgrimage to the Rainbow Bridge, John Shefford's heroic quest ends in the northern Painted Desert. On both levels the quest is successful. John and Fay, Jim and Jane return to Illinois to be with Bern Venters and Bess, completing that sense of community that usually ends the romantic's noble journey. They are reunited also with Black Star and Night, two of the equine scene stealers in *Riders of the Purple Sage*. And with the memory of deserts, mesas, canyons—and a towering stone bridge—Shefford returns to wholeness and peace.

✦

By 1915, the year that Harper's published both *The Lone Star Ranger* and *The Rainbow Trail,* Zane Grey was on his way to being not only an established writer, but a famous and wealthy one as well. *The Lone Star Ranger* made the best-seller lists; *The Rainbow Trail* was not far behind.[1] Mary Roberts Rinehart praised *The Rainbow Trail,* and Ripley Hitchcock of Harper's sent Grey a congratulatory letter. Dolly Grey called the book one of her husband's "thinking novels."[2]

Meanwhile, Grey's wanderlust continued. The previous year he had returned to Long Key and Catalina Island. He also visited the fishing grounds off Nova Scotia and New Jersey; he even got in a trip to the Navaho reservation in northern Arizona. The latter, however, was pure business, meant to confirm locations and verify customs and impressions.[3]

While Grey was riding the crest of popularity, other writers of western fiction were beginning to make their own voices heard. After the publication of *The Virginian* in 1902 and with Zane Grey's lead, the western story gained a wide audience. "Pulp" magazines flourished (called pulp because they were printed on cheap, unglazed newsprint). Writers of lesser talent than Grey tried to imitate him by using slick plots, stock characters, and exotic western settings. Writers like William Macleod Raine and Charles Olden Seltzer wrote this brand of lowbrow fiction, no doubt adding to the myth of the western superhero and perpetuating it through the first decades of the twentieth century. A host of pulp writers ground out hundreds of short stories for weekly, bimonthly, and monthly periodicals.

Max Brand (pseudonym of the very Teutonic-sounding Frederick Schiller Faust) appeared on the literary scene in 1917 as a twenty-five-year-old poet with a special affection for Italian Renaissance art. However, realizing that an attachment to art would keep him poor, he decided to emulate popular writers such as Zane Grey. Armed with a persuasive introduction letter, Faust stepped into the New York office of Robert Hobart Davis, a Grey friend and editor of *Munsey's* magazine. Davis glared at the upstart and snapped: "You're supposed to be able to write? Well, let's see if you can." Davis gave him a piece of paper. "Here's a plot. There's an empty room down the hall with a typewriter and a ream of paper in it. Go down there, if you like, and see if you can write a story. Third door on the right."

Davis thought that this was a sure-fire technique to winnow yet another greenhorn from the ranks of aspiring authors.

Faust took his instructions, banging away at the typewriter in the little room down the hall. Nearly seven hours later Faust emerged with a freshly-typed manuscript of close to a hundred pages. Davis was floored. It was a Herculean effort on Faust's part, and Davis knew it. Once more, it was good work.

"Where did you learn to write?" asked Davis.

Faust responded: "Third door on the right, down the hall."[4]

Actually, Frederick had been writing for several years, but the quip is pure Faustian bravado. And so began a career that for the next twenty-seven years produced a staggering quantity of novels, short fiction, essays, and screenplays.

The persona of Max Brand appeared around the time of his encounter with Davis. A friend suggested the idea that a good pen name consisted of two monosyllables with the same vowel sound in each.[5] Faust thought up Max Brand (partly to avoid using Frederick Faust during the anti-Germanic sentiment of World War I), and used it to create western fiction.

Although Brand graduated from the University of California at Berkeley, he did not find much in the West to interest him. Much of his writing was accomplished from his villa near Florence, Italy, where he "produced" book after book under seventeen different pen names. His youth (he was orphaned at thirteen) in Seattle and northern California was bitter and tragic, which no doubt prompted him to remark that the West was "disgusting."[6]

Despite caring little for the West, Brand mined its resources for popular, commercial fiction. His working methods were the opposite of Zane Grey's. Hoping to achieve the distance and timelessness of classical literature, he peopled his western fiction with heroes strictly from his imagination. He researched little, and cared nothing for accuracy of landscape and atmosphere. He wished to create myth, not paint a realistic portrayal of customs and routines in the West. Grey's research journeys through desert and forest would have exhausted and bored him.

In addition to writing, Brand had boundless appetites for wealth, romance, and learning. As "King of the Pulps" he managed to write several enduring titles in the genre: *The Untamed* (1919), *Destry Rides Again* (1930), *The Iron Trail* (1926), and *The Outlaw* (1933). Although his western novels provided him constant royalties, he groaned under the strained plots he had to use. "Daily, I thank God in three languages that I write under a pen name," he once admitted.[7]

Like Max Brand, Ernest Haycox endured a lonely childhood. Haycox was close to thirty years younger than Grey and wrote most of his best work after the latter's death in 1939. An Oregonian, Haycox served in the American army in France during World War I. After being mustered out, he returned to study at Reed College and the University of Oregon. Publishers' rejections of his writing at first were swift and plentiful, and he resorted to papering his walls with them.[8]

After studying Grey, Haycox began writing for the pulps and by 1931 had added three novels to his credit. These brought him some notoriety and he started writing for *Collier's* magazine, a move which boosted his reputation and insured him a career away from the pulps. Then came a handful of good novels that rounded out his career: *The Border Trumpet* (1939), *The Wild Bunch* (1943) and *The Earthbreakers* (1952). Haycox's startling imagery, economical prose, and intriguing characters endeared him to readers, many of whom place him at the head of the tradition.

A writer who reacted strongly to Grey's romantic storyline was Andy Adams, whose *Log of a Cowboy* (1903) was published the same year as *Betty Zane*. Adams had been a cowhand in Texas for many years before coming to Colorado during the Cripple Creek gold strike in 1891. After seeing Charles Hoyt's play *Texas Steer* in 1898, he was angered by its "ludicrous and false absurdities."[9] Thus began a steady and relentless literary campaign to set the record straight about the truth of western culture and to dismantle the large, unwieldy romantic tradition in general. Adams strove to write fiction "as convincingly as fact," stressing "authenticity, simplicity, and honesty."[10] As a consequence he loathed the Grey-Brand romances and dedicated his life to a realistic representation of the West.

When Emerson Hough published *Heart's Desire* in 1905, Andy Adams was one of the first to praise its authentic qualities. "The second winning of the West—for truth—is on," he wrote Hough, "and I extend my hand in congratulations."[11] Hough's early work tried for the realistic depictions expressed by Adams, but the more the lure of financial success called him the less he could hold on to his convictions about fidelity to authenticity. In short, romance's sweet song was more seductive that realism's grunts and groans.

Emerson Hough was close to Grey in height but built like a bulldog. While Grey suffered from chronic depression, Hough was afflicted with a nervous condition that interrupted his writing routine. The westward movement, particularly its effects on the conquerors and the conquered, continued to fascinate Hough all his life. *Heart's Desire* appeared before Grey had first traveled west, and for Hough its critical success helped congeal his rather erratic writing career. Like Grey, he was painstaking in his research. Hunting and fishing, too, were suitable peripheral activities on these trips. He wrote articles and short stories for *Century, Popular, Harper's Weekly,* and *The Saturday Evening Post.*

Hough's career culminated with two major works, *The Covered Wagon* (1922) and *North of '36* (1923). The former novel, with superb illustrations by W. H. D. Koerner, told of the pioneers crossing the plains in the mid-1800s, prompting Robert Stewart of *McCall's* to call it "the greatest story of the winning of the West yet written."[12] It was made into a successful film in 1923, directed by James Cruze, and it was quickly recognized as the first epic western movie. *North of '36* traces the actions of the first trail herd to be driven from Texas to Kansas, and like *The Covered Wagon*, it was made into a critically acclaimed film. *North of '36* featured the acting talents of Noah Beery, Lois Wilson, and Jack Holt.

Outside the western romance genre but still part of the literary movement in the American West were writers such as Jack London, Hamlin Garland, and Willa Cather. London and Grey, nearly contemporary in age, both revered the ideas of Herbert Spencer, and London felt urged to give the philosopher overt recognition in such works as *The Sea Wolf* (1904). Grey, however, called Ernest Seton and Jack London "pure fakes, as far as animals go. What they write is as the President said—a closet product."[13] London was hardly "a closet product." It would be difficult to select an American writer with a more adventurous and curious spirit than London, but Grey sometimes harbored resentments for no clear reason.

Farm life on the western prairies continued to be probed and analyzed by artists like Hamlin Garland and Willa Cather. Paling in comparison with the vivid exploits of a Jack Hare or a Jim Lassiter, a Hamlin Garland character inhabits a world of routine, hardship, loneliness, and death. Grey admired Garland, though, no doubt for the strength and endurance of his characters in a harsh land.

Willa Cather came to prominence with *O Pioneers!* in 1913, when Grey was still enjoying the financial rewards of *Riders of the Purple Sage*. Although she traveled throughout the world and absorbed a keen sense of its spirit, she felt rooted in Nebraska, setting some of her most successful novels there: *The Song of the Lark* (1915), *One of Ours* (1922), and *The Lost Lady* (1923). Cather's novels of surprising beauty, subdued action, and provocative characters contrast with Grey's books of violent duels and sere wastelands, but both writers could agree on their emotional ties to the soil.

When World War I broke out in Europe in 1914, many Americans thought it would be a strictly regional conflict that would not involve the United States. But as ground offensive followed ground offensive, after three years of interminable trench warfare, the war had settled into a stalemate. Each side took enormous losses, sometimes within a period of three days. The romantic age symbolized by Victorian and Edwardian England—the era that Zane and Dolly had both come of age in—was falling apart. It had been a world of genteel society, college prep schools and universities, of fraternities and sororities, of rowing down the Delaware and playing baseball. It was an age of safety and security, when the only war—the Spanish-American War of 1898—turned into a quick and decisive victory for the United States. Then, a brash upstart named Teddy Roosevelt helped rout the Spanish in Cuba. There were no heroes in this European war, only a constant clashing of armies in the mud of France.

For Grey the war years of 1914–18 were particularly difficult, punctuated by severe depression, family worries, abusive critics, and feelings of helplessness amid a European crisis that seemed on the edge of a holocaust. With casualty figures mounting and war's weary gloom appearing in newspaper headlines, Americans by 1917 had begun to feel the conflict's psychological and emotional reverberations. Grey wrote that he "felt like an atom whirling in a universe of winds."[14] He turned to authors like Tennyson and Stevenson for inspiration in these times. On Wordsworth he reflected: "'The world is too much with us' and 'where is the glory and the dream?' of yesterday, he meant, of flower and the beauty of life that has gone! Something dark and gloomy borders my spirit. I must work and move about, and cease brooding . . ."[15]

To assuage his feelings Grey hurled himself into his writing, or quietly slipped away to fish or hunt. Or frequently he engaged in self-pity, lashing out at those around him, or other famous authors. Overly sensitive and painfully shy, he continued to absorb since childhood an undue amount of shame and guilt that festered into gloom and self-punishment.

Grey had continued to abstain from alcohol during these years. It is very likely that, given the severity of his depression, had he used liquor in quantities to alleviate pain he might have aggravated the problem and ultimately destroyed his career. Writing, sometimes at a hectic pace, was the antidote to depression. So in an odd sense, the depression drove him to and kept him at the writing table, thus ensuring the continuity and health of his livelihood.

Throughout the war Grey maintained an ardent anti-German position, disliking the Germans' warmongering attitude and their fanaticism and authoritarianism. He was glad in a way that he could help the Americans upon their entry into the war in 1917. His books became the favorites of American soldiers overseas.[16] Grey's contemporary, William Raine, also fared well in the European theater. The British government bought five hundred thousand copies of Raine's works to supply the "tommies" at the front.[17]

Meanwhile, Grey's career was steadily ascending. *The Border Legion* appeared in 1916, and the serialization of *Wildfire* in *Country Gentleman* in April 1916 signaled that his life in the pulps was nearly over and that his new one in the "serious" periodicals had begun. Frank Tenney Johnson did the illustrations, his first commission in a major magazine.

Although not in the same echelon with *Harper's, Scribner's* or *Century, Country Gentleman* was a respectable journal that was closing in on a circulation of half a million per week. Its targeted audience was "the old, rural individualistic and humanistic America that was fast crumbling before the onslaughts of industrialization."[18] Grey's values matched the editors', and so began a long, fruitful relationship between author and periodical.[19]

One of the reasons that Grey gained preeminence during the second decade of the twentieth century was that he began a careful, even systematic, campaign to build and sustain a legacy. From *The Heritage of the Desert* in 1910 through *Wildfire* in 1917, Grey chose each setting and time frame with strategic precision: *Heritage* (historical; mountain-desert; southern Utah); *Desert Gold* (contemporary; desert; southern Arizona); *Riders of the Purple Sage* (historical; mountain-desert; southern Utah); *The Light of Western Stars* (contemporary; desert-prairie; New Mexico); *The Lone Star Ranger* (historical; prairie; Texas); *The Rainbow Trail* (historical; mountain-desert; northern Arizona–southern Utah); *The Border Legion* (historical; mountains; Idaho); *Wildfire* (historical; canyons; northern Arizona). Added to this Grey varied plot, structure, and characterization to create a comprehensive and rich tapestry of western life with each new novel.

With the book *Wildfire,* however, Grey injects an important variation into his strategy. He introduces a horse as protagonist. By placing the horse in the role ordinarily reserved for human heroes he attracts the reader's sympathies and assures the emotional focus. London achieved this magnificently with Buck in *The Call of the Wild.* Grey creates a truly Herculean image in Wildfire, but seems unable, or unwilling, to sustain the novel's charm through to the end. The two horses, Sage King and Wildfire, are pursued by a "wild fire" or grass blaze started by the villain. The book climaxes with the violent death of Wildfire, who, "choked, blinded, dying, killed on his feet," collapses and dies. Rather than creating pathos, Grey writes a scene of repulsive and gratuitous violence. A hero has fallen, but there is no wisdom or clarity that issues from the death: only waste and desolation. Grey did not repeat this pattern with his human heroes, which makes *Wildfire* a unique—and tragic—exception to his customary endings.

As early as 1916, Grey learned from Harper and Brothers that motion picture tycoon William Fox was interested in purchasing the rights to *Riders of the Purple Sage.*[20] Grey met Fox in New York City where the latter offered the author $2,500 for picture rights for *Riders.* Grey at first was cautious. After Fox added another $2,500 for *The Light of Western Stars,* Grey seized the deal. Thus began an association between Zane Grey and Hollywood that would add one more important dimension to Grey's legacy as a novelist.

12

The Silver Screen

Clearly and simply, the dovetailing of Zane Grey's writing career with the rising popularity of cinema not only insured his place in western fiction but also allowed him worldwide success. Grey's novels were naturally suited to the fledgling motion picture industry. Stressing action and romantic settings with subordinate dialogue, they could easily make the transition from page to screen and retain their freshness and power. On screen his chaste, petite, independent women contrasted with his tough, laconic men. As a backdrop, the mesas, mountains, and spurs—symbols of the permanence and beauty of the American West—rose in silent splendor around them. In short, his romances were eminently filmable and packaged for a receptive audience who could experience the West in the smoky, flickering darkness of a Saturday matinee.

The western movie had a short but successful history before it arrived in Grey's ken. Buttressed by the huge popularity of the western dime novel, the first true western film, *Cripple Creek Barroom*, appeared in 1898. Eastern audiences gobbled up the action in this brief vignette. In 1903 Edwin S. Porter's *The Great Train Robbery* was produced, introducing two key concepts into filmmaking of the West: a continuous narrative with a beginning, middle, and end; and the formula of crime-chase-punishment, which would prevail throughout the westerns of the subsequent period.[1] Shot on location in the "wilds" of New Jersey, the picture lasted only ten minutes, but it was the keystone of all ensuing western films.

By 1910 (significantly, the year *The Heritage of the Desert* appeared) moviemaking operations were being relocated from New Jersey to Hollywood. Southern California offered a better climate and more appropriate scenery for shooting westerns. The move to California spawned new careers of two notable figures: D. W. Griffith, the great director, and G. M. "Broncho" Billy Anderson, the first western star. During this time the stratification of "B" and "A" westerns began to emerge. B (budget) films were hastily produced for mass audiences and often presented a distorted, exaggerated view of the West.

However, the escapist features of the B western cannot be overlooked. During the war years particularly they provided audiences with a quick, cheap, action-filled diversion from the anxieties of daily life. On the other hand, their poor camera work, deficient film quality, jerky action, and bad editing made them difficult—even embarrassing—to watch. These limitations, however, did not affect their popularity.[2] The more serious A pictures took more time to shoot and awaited the support of more generous producers.

The B's, for all their detractors, helped crystallize the essential elements of the western mythos. Applauded by kids in darkened movie theaters and chided by critics in newspaper columns, the B's accompanied Hollywood into its Golden Age in the late 1930s and early 1940s.

In 1911 motion picture pioneers Samuel Goldfish (later Goldwyn), Cecil B. De Mille, and Jesse L. Lasky acquired the rights to *The Squaw Man,* an acclaimed Broadway play. Filming was to begin outdoors in New Jersey. However, the tenacious eastern winter did not permit them an early start. Hearing that Arizona winters might allow them a more comfortable shoot, Lasky and lead actor William Farnum headed to Flagstaff to begin the filming. Flagstaff, however, was in the grip of a blizzard when they arrived. The two continued on to Hollywood, shot the film, edited it, and released it from California, making it the first movie to be completed on the West Coast. Lasky would go on to be the inspiration for Paramount Studios and a good friend of Grey's in the industry.[3] De Mille would become a successful director of epics, while Samuel Goldwyn became the catalyst behind Metro-Goldwyn-Mayer studios.

When D. W. Griffith's *Birth of a Nation* appeared in 1915 Hollywood was no longer a fledgling producer of movies but a bustling center of filmmaking. Independent studios were created overnight. Directors, producers, cameramen, actors, and gaffers streamed in from the east, including a twenty-two-year-old stagehand named Sean Aloysius O'Feeney—later known as John Ford, one of the premier directors of westerns.[4]

Actors were achieving status as well. In 1916—the year Grey sold two novels to William M. Fox—William S. Hart starred in *Hell's Hinges* and gave stability, poise, and realism to the early western movie. Hart had made several one- and two-reel features, but with *Hell's Hinges* he helped create a western that would influence a whole generation of filmmakers. Just a little over a year older than Zane Grey, William S. Hart at forty-five years of age had capped a diverse career in pictures with this movie. Unlike many actors, directors, and writers, Hart knew the West, having been a roustabout and cowboy in Kansas early in his career. Rejecting the frothy sentimentalism of the era, Hart as director and actor brought dignity and psychological depth to the Western hero. "The truth of the West," wrote Hart, echoing Andy Adams, "meant more to me than a job, and always will." Hart's career endured through the twenties, when Grey's western features were in their heyday.

Almost from the day he signed his first movie contracts, Grey was entranced by the idea of having his romances on screen. Actual film work did not begin on them until May 1918. Fox cameramen worked in

Jess Smith *(left)*, Jack Moore *(center)*, and Zane Grey *(right)* on location in Red Lake, Arizona, c. 1925, during the filming of *Wild Horse Mesa*. As a writer and producer, Grey was one of the pioneers of the Hollywood western. *Courtesy of the G. M. Farley Collection, Hagerstown, Maryland*

northern Arizona filming background material, amid the rising heat and sporadic duststorms.

Meanwhile, Grey made a crucial decision. The demands of the motion picture business, combined with his love for California ocean fishing, affected his choice of the West Coast as his permanent home. The train ride from Lackawaxen to California took five days one-way. The necessity of monitoring the production of his films and the additional lure of Avalon harbor on Catalina outweighed his deep affection for the rivers and trails around Lackawaxen. The Greys retained their house in Pennsylvania, while moving to southern California, eventually settling in a Spanish house in Altadena, near Los Angeles. Romer was now nine, Betty six, and Loren, born in 1915, was approaching three.[5]

Once settled near Hollywood, Grey plunged into his new-found love—the Silver Screen and its attendant froth. After Fox produced *Riders of the Purple Sage* and *The Light of Western Stars,* Grey decided to form his own movie company and retain money from ticket sales.

Consequently, he founded Zane Grey Productions in association with Benjamin H. Hampton, who oversaw production while Grey monitored scripts.[6]

Over the next several years, Zane Grey Productions made seven motion pictures, Grey being adamant about several key features of movie production. First he maintained that his company film location shots that were mentioned in his books, or as close to them as possible. This fidelity of movie to novel was paramount with Grey. Second, he believed the actors and actresses should subordinate themselves to the roles they were playing and not seek stardom. The "star" concept bothered Grey because it challenged his views on humility and self-deprecation. "Your elimination of the star system is going to revolutionize the motion picture business," he wrote. "Just so long as stars insist on having all the strong scenes of a book, just so long motion pictures will be weak."[7] Of course Hollywood shattered Grey's unrealistic expectations and eventually he castigated the industry's people and products.

In 1919, however, Grey had no such ideas about motion pictures; he was eager to prove himself. That year his company filmed *Desert Gold* near Palm Springs, California. He eagerly told his partner Hampton: "You have put the spirit, the action, and the truth of *Desert Gold* upon the screen."[8]

Between 1918 and 1922 Zane Grey Productions filmed such later Grey titles as *The U.P. Trail* and *The Man of the Forest*. At one point, Grey even considered moving operations to Arizona, but later thought better of it.[9] By 1922, exasperated by Hollywood's lack of ethics, Grey decided to buy Hampton's share and sell out to Jesse L. Lasky of Paramount Pictures, who years before had guided *The Squaw Man* into a successful film.

Grey found in Lasky a kindred spirit, and Paramount Pictures treated Grey's work with respect and dignity. Lasky and Paramount were to produce fifty-four movies from the Grey novels (including several remakes). Between 1922 and 1929 Paramount contracts stipulated that filming take place on the actual locations of the book. Grey received $25,000 for the film rights to each novel and often served as advisor on the set.

As audiences increased and budgets swelled in the early 1920s, movie shooting locations took on the characteristics of epic western pictures. Most cameras and lighting equipment had to be hauled from Flagstaff to northern Arizona by horse and mule train. Tent cities for the actors and actresses mushroomed on the cactus and sage valleys. Corrals and barns were erected near the shooting sites. Hundreds of horses were conscripted from nearby ranches to use in filming. Motion picture crews probably spent more time in the northern high desert battling the sun, rain, and fierce wind than they did on Hollywood tennis courts.

Paramount retained numerous stars of the early silent movies for Grey stories, among them Richard Dix and Noah Beery Sr., both of whom starred in *The Heritage of the Desert.* Directors Victor Fleming (later to direct *Gone With the Wind*) and John Huston began their careers in the Arizona deserts, most notably directing Grey material for the screen.

The filming of *The Heritage of the Desert* in late 1923 was a typical massive operation for film crews of the 1920s. Shooting took place near Lee's Ferry on the Colorado River, involving seventy crew members, fifty Indians, and two thousand horses.[10] While filming was proceeding, Grey toured Arizona with Jesse Lasky scouting other locations. Grey continued to be pleased with Paramount's handling of his romances.

The filming of Emerson Hough's *The Covered Wagon* in 1923 introduced the lavish-scale western, raising the standard expected by both movie companies and audiences. Consequently, Grey's movies after that year, though still "silent," tended to be grander, with larger budgets. Locations were chosen with deliberation. Budgets rose to half a million and later to a million dollars per film. Large productions such as Grey's *The Vanishing American* were delayed more than a year because of cost overruns. *The Vanishing American,* Grey's 1925 novel, was directed by George B. Seitz (originally Victor Fleming was to direct) and filmed near Kayenta, the Rainbow Bridge, and Tuba City.[11]

In scope, sensitivity, and characterization, *The Vanishing American* was perhaps Grey's greatest screen achievement.

While Paramount was "growing" a crop of stars for Grey pictures, Fox studios was trying to keep pace. The latter rushed a young Tom Mix into a remake of *Riders of the Purple Sage.* In his prodigious sombrero and pressed bandanna, Mix seemed an unlikely choice for the somber lead role. Other contradictions occurred with the script, which called for Mix to play a Texas Ranger. The Mormon angle was totally missing, resulting in a movie that resembled the book only in name. Tom Mix also starred in Fox's *The Rainbow Trail,* in which he was cast as Shefford. Again, the film departed so drastically from the book that any similarity was purely coincidental. Because Grey did not have authorial control over Fox properties, the studio executives and writers gave free rein to their imaginations.

This heedless pirating of his material no doubt prompted Grey in 1927 to claim he would "not say that all people in Hollywood are crooks, but [he would say] that all crooks in Hollywood are in the motion picture industry." By that time Paramount was taking excessive liberties with settings and characters. Grey's prolific output was catching up with him. The sheer volume of his words, and anyone's desire to capitalize on them and his name, made it impossible any longer to ensure fidelity or accuracy in the translation of his work from page to screen.

By 1928 the silent film was on the verge of becoming an anachronism. With the coming of sound pictures, Grey more and more retreated from his involvement with the studios. Fewer films were being shot on location, and a huge crop of B movies was being released by independent studios. Grey finally realized that the more his work was popularized in films the more it diluted and destroyed his original concepts of the West.

Although part of his heart was in moviemaking, Grey's soul was in writing and controlling all aspects of the creative process. His power lay in his ability to create a sense—a spirit—of place, and while movie industry people were indifferent to this, Grey knew it was his salvation.

13

Stranger on the Golden Shore

When Grey moved to southern California in 1918, his extended family
—brothers R.C. and Ellsworth—packed up and migrated with Dolly,
Zane, and the children. His sister Ida remained with their mother at
Lackawaxen. That year he also bought three acres of land on the rim of
the Grand Canyon and eventually had a cabin built on it. Once in California the brothers remained close, R.C. and Ellsworth often stopping
at the Greys' to play cards and chat. Zane was forty-six and gray had
begun to streak his thatched hair.

With the psychological and physical break from the east coast, Grey
explored new themes in his work. Nineteen eighteen saw the publication of *The U.P. Trail*, a sprawling epic novel in the mode of Rex
Beach, about the building of the Union Pacific railroad, and Grey's
first true historical western novel.[1]

In this brawny, action-oriented tale, Grey relates the events in
Wyoming and Nebraska in the years 1866–1869, and the final driving of
the golden spike in Utah. Wishing to recreate the "epical turmoil" (in

the words of Robert Louis Stevenson) of the era, Grey plunged into historical research and borrowed the rest from his trail buddy, Al Doyle. As a result, *The U.P. Trail* is a more realistic novel than *Riders of the Purple Sage* and is Grey's best novel since 1912.

For this story to succeed as historical fiction, Grey needed to depart from the customary features of romance. He abandoned the desert and oasis in favor of the low Wyoming foothills with the thread of track bed running to the horizon. Grey also took some delight in describing the railroad town of Benton, a departure that is significant in Zane Grey's work since he loathed cities. Most of his early novels contain nothing of town life, only the vacant lands surrounding it. Drowsy Mormon hamlets are described, but never towns with banks and offices and saloons and people scurrying about.

Benton, in the red desert country of western Wyoming, is the logistical center for Union Pacific railroad operations. Consequently, it attracts the best and worst of men and women brought to the Rockies to put the rail lines through. Its bawdy, rollicking main street contains its share of bars and gambling houses and its knots of liquored, restless men; as "hub of the railway universe," Benton pulsates with "the sting and wildness of life."

> Beyond Medicine Bow the grass and the green failed and the immense train of freight-cars and passenger-coaches, loaded to capacity, clattered on into arid country. Gray and red, the drab and fiery colors of the desert lent the ridges character—forbidding and barren. . . .
>
> It lay in the heart of barrenness, alkali, and desolation, on the face of the windy desert, alive with dust-devils, sweeping along, yellow and funnel-shaped—a huge blocked-out town, and set where no town could ever live. Benton was prey for sun, wind, dust, drought, and the wind was terribly and insupportably cold. No sage, no grass, not even a cactus-bush, nothing green or living to relieve the eye, which swept across the gray and the white, through the dust, to the distant bare and desolate hills of drab.
>
> The hell that was reported to abide at Benton was in harmony with its setting. (p. 158)

Benton, like Cottonwoods in *Riders of the Purple Sage*, is dying. As the line moves farther and farther west, the need for a permanent base becomes unnecessary. Grey poignantly reveals the slow death: "Like a mushroom it had arisen, and like a dust storm on the desert wind it had roared away, bearing the freight of labor, of passion, and of evil. Benton had become a name—a fabulous name."

As the Irish work gangs press west, as the rails slice through the heart of Sioux territory, and as the buffalo decline in number, Grey describes the death of an era, a landscape, and a people. But Grey's story is how new life forces itself through winter's deadness. Warren Neale, a roustabout New Englander, climbs the ranks of burly railroadmen, who are furiously trying to push the railroad west to hook up with Chinese work gangs laying track from California. Neale is ambitious and, like Grey, an opportunist. Complicating his ascent in the world is Allie Lee, a young woman left for dead in a Sioux raid, whom Neale takes under his wing. Predictably, they fall in love and the rest of the novel is largely devoted to revealing how Neale and Allie Lee find, lose, and ultimately rediscover each other amid the clamor of events.

Neale and Allie Lee, symbols of the emerging West, are more able to accept the disruptions and deal with the West's inevitable changes. On the other hand, Slingerland, the mountain man, unable to witness the destruction of his beloved West, turns remorsefully to the sanctity of the Rockies. Neale embraces commerce and its attendant problems. Allie Lee does too. While the old life disintegrates around them, a new one is forged for them in Promontory Point, Utah. As the two Union Pacific lines are merged in the desert, Allie slips her hand into Neale's, symbolizing the human promise of connection and love within the scope of more important convergences. Actually, it rained heavily the day the final spike was driven. But Grey would have none of that. The sun gleams as brightly on the ceremony as the golden spike did in the hearts of the men who forged a link across the continent.

The novel contains a host of colorful, salty, maverick characters, including the redoubtable flagman Casey, who toward the end of the novel single-handedly drives a train into Sioux territory. In a remarkable tour-de-force, Grey portrays Casey as a comical but hard-nosed Irishman. The train ride is one of the memorable parts of the novel, largely because Grey allows Casey enough frailty that the reader can both cheer his heroism and empathize with his shortcomings. Since the author's main characters rarely (if ever) have this weakness, any traces of it in minor characters hold some promise for Grey as a versatile novelist.

Almost completely devoid of Grey's belief in Social Darwinism, or of any philosophy for that matter, *The U.P. Trail* is one of Grey's best novels, simply because it can tell a story and recreate an era with minimal intrusion by the author. Grey dedicated the novel to Ripley Hitchcock, his friend and early nemesis at Harper and Brothers. However, it is Robert Louis Stevenson who is Grey's inspiration and the driving spirit of the book. Grey learned from Stevenson how to eliminate himself and let the theme of the book be communicated through action, deed, and dialogue. Of course it was an additional bonus that Stevenson had traveled in the American West and written of his experiences on the Union Pacific Railroad in the late 1870s. *The U.P. Trail* is evidence that Grey learned well from his mentor.

The clash of departure and emergence, of death and new life, of permanence and change, of cynicism and optimism forms the tension of *The U.P. Trail;* these were also the forces that tore at Grey as a person and novelist. On one hand he is the young, zestful Warren Neale, ready to take on the West; on the other, anticipating his later years and the decline of the West, he is Slingerland, who returns to the isolation and protection of the wilderness. The book ends with Slingerland's vision predominant. Like the Sioux, he views the railroads and the trails west with grim suspicion, acknowledging that a way of life is "vanishing—vanishing—vanishing." It is a book that Grey could have written only in midlife, when the pain of experience had tempered some of his youthful bravado.

The publication of *The U.P. Trail* marked a crucial point in Zane Grey's career: its success helped Grey decide to continue to write westerns and adventure stories only. He wrote to Hitchcock at Harper's that "much good has come to me ... since *The U.P. Trail* was published. It is like wine." To a woman friend he wrote: "All these years my idea has been to win a public, and then write the powerful psychological novels of love, passion, and tragedy that I am capable of writing." If it was simply a question of will power, Grey could have been in a league with Hawthorne or Kipling. He simply did not have the talent, the tools, or the preparation for such ambitions. He did try to project this aspiration to the world, however, particularly when the critics hounded him about a particular project and he tried to soothe himself by saying that he was capable of loftier goals. But in his heart he knew his limitations. In February 1918 he jotted in his diary: "My power and my study and passion shall be directed to that which already I have written best—the beauty and color and mystery of great spaces, of the open, of Nature in her wild moods. This decision has been a relief."[2]

The U.P. Trail headed the best-seller lists in 1918 and helped make Grey one of the wealthiest authors in America.[3] Additionally in that year, *Field and Stream* serialized Grey's paean to fishing "Gladiators of the Sea" and "Avalon the Beautiful"—both published in book form in 1919 as *Tales of Fishes.* Moreover, *Country Gentleman* (May 4, 1918) was serializing Grey's new novel, *The Desert of Wheat*—illustrated by Koerner—in which Grey described the confrontations between wheat farmers and the International Workmen of the World during World War I in the Bend country of Washington state.

The Great War changed Grey's thinking, and nowhere is it more evident than in *The Desert of Wheat.* In it he departed dramatically from the cowboy-lawman-desperado themes of his early work and concentrated on raising awareness about contemporary issues. If nothing else, the war gave Grey a sense of suffering, not only of his countrymen, but of all peoples. Suffering provided Grey insight and compassion, and it also made him angry enough to voice his opinions about it.

The Desert of Wheat takes place just after America's entry into the war in 1917. Grey's view of Germany, which passed from suspicion in 1914 to outright hatred toward the end of the war, is tempered in the person of Kurt Dorn, the main character. Kurt is torn between obeying his German-born father and serving his country in the U.S. army at the front. His neighbors try to convince him that he can best serve his country by remaining at home on the farm. The heroine, Lenore Anderson, is equally troubled by her conflicting motives and emotions.

> Dorn would go to war as no ordinary soldier, to obey, to fight, to do his duty; but for some strange, unfathomable obsession of his own. And, therefore, if he went at all he was lost. War, in its inexplicable horror, killed the souls of endless hordes of men. Therefore, if he went at all she, too, was lost to the happiness that might have been hers. She would never love another man. She could never marry. She would never have a child.
>
> So his soul and her happiness were in the balance weighed against a woman's power. It seemed to Lenore that she felt hopelessly unable to carry the issue to victory; and yet, on the other hand, a tumultuous and wonderful sweetness of sensation called to her, insidiously, of the infallible potency of love. What could she do to save Dorn's life and his soul? There was only one answer to that. She would do anything. She must make him love her to the extent that he would have no will to carry out this desperate intent. There was little time to do that. The gradual growth of affection through intimacy and understanding was not possible here. It must come as a flash of lightning. She must bewilder him with the revelation of her love, and then by all its incalculable power hold him there. (p. 211)

But Dorn, in a crisis of conscience, joins anyway, serves in France, is wounded, and returns to America, his body and mind shattered by war.

Lenore Anderson is modeled on Dolly Grey, who sets the standard for Zane's women. Lenore nurses Dorn to health and mental wholeness, marries him, and becomes his major emotional supporter. In an early draft of the manuscript, Grey declared that women "were cursed with lesser bodies [than men] and blessed with higher souls." If war, according to Grey, proved to be an example of the survival of the fittest for men, it was more abhorrent to women because they had to sacrifice their children to it. Grey deleted these ideas from the final manuscript. However, seeking a solution to the end of war, he proposed something close to the aims of the women in the Greek comedy *Lysistrata*. Women should unite and refuse to have children, thus ensuring "an end to violence, to greed, to hate, to war . . ."[4]

Like many writers during and after the Great War, Grey felt impelled to record the conflict's horrifying effects and offer his own remedies. When to everyone's gratitude the war wound down to an exhausted whimper in November 1918, Grey was quick to vent his relief and anger: "Right has prevailed over the Brute. . . . Germans should not pay in gold—but in blood."[5] It took Grey several years to shed his antagonism toward Germany, convinced as he was that only by heaping war guilt upon her could another disaster be prevented.

In January 1919 Zane took a break from writing and spearheading Zane Grey Productions to travel through Death Valley with fishing chum-turned-prospector Sievert Nielsen. A strapping vagabond, the 35-year-old Nielsen accompanied Grey on several adventures in Arizona and California.[6] For several days Nielsen and Grey probed the wastes of one of the hottest, driest, and most desolate places on earth.[7] The vast emptiness and rising temperatures tormented him and propelled him on. Grey felt urged to travel through Death Valley, as if in completing this mythic journey he was really trying to resolve an inner struggle and to understand the depths of his own isolation. Like so many spiritual pilgrims, he chose the desert to connect with his elusive spirituality.

Death Valley proved a drastic departure from his other wanderings. The deserts of northern and southern Arizona were barren also, but not as lifeless as this lonely, shifting plain, where the only signs of motion were the scuttlings of a scorpion or the whirlings of a sand devil on the dunes. In camp and on the trail, Grey felt a new novel germinating, one that would bring him back to the desert.[8]

After Grey returned to Hollywood, he began work on *Wanderer of the Wasteland,* his most autobiographical and enigmatic book, and one that would have a tempestuous, passionate, and writhing birth. The actual writing took him five months, marked by a furious bout with his emotions. He realized that depression hovered over him at the beginning of any project, and so he drew up a plan. "This novel," he wrote, "will not be great unless I have absolute control and restraint; and I am absolutely determined that it will be a great novel. I must look out for nervous strain. I must not hurry. I must not try to do too much in a short time. . . . I must be prepared to expect depressions and to understand them, and to meet them with intelligence and counteraction, with change and will."[9] Nearly a month later, in February, he was turning to writers like John Ruskin and Matthew Arnold (particularly his poem "Dover Beach") for inspiration. Grey noted: "I shall take time with this great book. It grows and grows. . . . I shall utterly spend myself, my passion and soul on it before I finish." Four days later he admitted: "Today I am sore, angry, bitter, and hopeless . . . the mood lingers. . . . I had the most trying time, sitting here, making scratches on my manuscript."[10]

He returned to Death Valley in March, partly to revisit the landscape and partly to get a spark of inspiration. Upon returning home he wrote, "I walked across that ghastly place and back again. There has been too much delay and abstraction in the course of my writing *Wanderer of the Wasteland,* some of it necessary and much of it needless."[11]

As if achieving an epiphany about his intense work habits, Grey, toward the end of April, noted: "Surely yesterday I was slated for the blues. But I determined not to succumb. I have established a fact. Many years has this been coming. Work is my salvation. It changes my moods."[12] As the manuscript pages piled up, Grey drove himself mercilessly towards the finish. "I have worked harder for two days. My eyes ache, my hand is numbed, my arms feel dead."[13] Grey completed the manuscript—"eight hundred and thirty-eight pages, one hundred and seventy thousand words"—toward the end of May. "It is midnight," he scrawled in his diary. "I have just ended my novel Wanderer of the Wasteland . . . and I sweat blood."[14]

Grey promptly sold the serial rights to *McClure's* (beginning May 1920); the Harper and Brothers clothbound edition was published in 1923. Not since John Hare in *Heritage of the Desert* had Grey created a character (Adam Larey) who was so much like him.

On the surface, *Wanderer* appears similar to other Grey quest novels such as *The Heritage of the Desert* and *The Rainbow Trail* because the plot and characters seem part of the Grey formula. The action takes place in southern Arizona, near Yuma, and eventually spreads into the Mojave Desert and Death Valley, some two hundred miles to the northwest. Adam Larey, a drifter, thinking he has killed his brother Guerd, escapes into the desert. Unaccustomed to the inferno, Adam quickly loses strength and the will to live. He is found and nursed to health by a prospector named Dismukes. The two begin a lasting friendship, with Dismukes becoming Adam's mentor and guide. Adam eventually strikes out on his own, first staying with Indians in the Chocolate Mountains and then wandering across the Mojave towards Death Valley, where he sojourns with Magdalena and Elliot Virey, two desert sorts whose cabin is imperiled by an avalanche waiting to happen. Assuming a new identity, Adam becomes "Wansfell the Wanderer," condemned forever to atone for his brother's death and tramp the wasteland.

All this sounds familiar, but it is the allegory which becomes intriguing. One question is overwhelming: why did Grey have such a tormenting experience with the writing of *Wanderer of the Wasteland*? One answer seems appropriate: because he was writing his own story, using his familiar symbols to tell it.[15]

Simply put, *Wanderer of the Wasteland* is Grey's autobiography with a variety of plot turns and settings inserted for interest. Having killed his father's dream for him (to become a dentist and live in the East), Grey turns to the unknown to become a writer. Only by destroying his father's dream can he have one of his own. He changes the spelling of his last name. He stumbles at first, unsure of himself, feeling guilty in his own arrogance. By himself he knows he will die. Slowly he gathers support, first from Dolly, then from a series of mentors (Buffalo Jones, Jim Emmett, Al Doyle), who not only nourish him but provide him answers to the meaning of existence. The writer becomes drawn to the desert, knowing that it is full of pain but replete with meaning. He creates characters who enter it, subdue it, and achieve enlightenment. He spends his life in search of the same enlightenment; at times he swells with knowledge; other times he is thwarted; still other times he is utterly defeated. Like Adam, the writer presses on, a wanderer in the wasteland, a pilgrim stumbling through the awful reality of daily existence. Adam becomes an irrational rescuer. He tries to soothe others' pain, so he in turn can be soothed by them. Like his character, the writer becomes a needy little boy in the desert, searching out things and people to relieve his pain.

Beyond its allegorical content, however, *Wanderer* is simply good storytelling, revealing Grey's long background in developing a novel. The book contains some diverse influences, among them the Bible, Joseph Conrad, and Matthew Arnold. The Cain-Abel association is strong throughout the novel; Adam is thrust naked into the world, traveling about doing simple acts of goodness to atone for his deed. The plot is set in motion by circumstances similar to those of Joseph Conrad's *Lord Jim*: a man overwhelmed by a single moment of poor moral judgment spends years seeking redemption. Like Conrad's Jim, Adam Larey becomes an outcast hoping to show the world his true goodness. His wanderings become a savage quest to reconcile nature and God and ultimately to find wisdom and serenity in a universe of tragedy, indifference, and chaos.

Zane Grey identified with Conrad's lost souls wandering through exotic ports and jungles. With Arnold he shared an agony about the need to accept new scientific principles such as Darwinism and the desire to attain religious certainty. Arnold, writing in mid-Victorian England, demonstrated his pain in such poems as "Dover Beach," which Grey perused while plodding through *Wanderer*. While listening to the sea ebbing, Arnold hears Christianity receding with it, until he hears only "its melancholy, long, withdrawing roar, / Retreating, to the breath / or the night wind, down the vast edges drear / And the naked shingles of the world." Arnold's image of "naked shingles . . . stone beaches" appealed deeply to Grey, as did the poet's cynicism. Adam Larey, in a moment of immobilizing pain, feels the insignificance of man in a tragic, indifferent universe:

> His hope, his prayer, his frailty, his fall, his burden and agony and life—these were nothing to the desert that worked inscrutably through its millions of years . . . but a spirit as illimitable and as inscrutable breathed out of the universe and over the immensity of desert space . . . and bade him rise and take up his burden and go on down the naked shingles of the world. (p. 113)

As Grey survived in a harsh world, so too Adam learns to overcome paralysis by sheer will power and action: "Despair and pride and fear of death, and this strange breath of life, dragged Adam up and drove him down the desert road." Simply surviving, however, will not sustain Adam—he yearns for religious experience and peace. As the desert roads lengthen and the sun grows hotter, he feels that he, like Romantic poets, is merging with the desert elements. "Oh, stars," he cries, "so serene and pitiless and inspiring—teach me to perform the tasks as you perform yours." Instead of being a mere witness to experience, Adam seeks oneness and harmony with the sun, sand, and meandering scorpion. This mystical union, however, is nearly always just out of Adam's reach, as he struggles with earthly guilt, shame, and fear.

Three of Grey's scarlet literary sins were perpetuating formulaic plots, injecting heightened emotionalism into commonplace experiences, and creating characters who were notorious "boundary crashers." Although these features continue in *Wanderer of the Wasteland*, they are not as apparent, probably because Grey's narrative skill has become developed to its highest degree. But Adam still possesses the customary flaw of the Grey romantic hero. He is quite willing to venture a great distance into Death Valley because Dismukes thinks that a white woman living there won't be able to withstand the summer heat. From this point in the novel, his choice is predictable. The slightest hint of a person—particularly a young woman—imperiled gets men digging out their suits of armor and saddling their moon-white chargers. Most often this ends in romance and spiritual union, the together-ness-is-next-to-godliness syndrome of Shelley and Tennyson.

In *Wanderer* there are some old-fashioned lines such as: "Have you not learned that the grandest act on earth is when a man fights for the honor or love or happiness or life of woman?" The reader who can look beyond this will discover Grey's ability to create an atmosphere— of both the awful beauty and harshness of the Mojave and the stark psychological terror it provokes. At the end of the novel Adam Larey meets a miner named Merryvale who tells him that his brother, Guerd, is not really dead. Adam, it seems, only grazed him with a bullet fourteen years before. " 'You've hid in the desert,' " says Merryvale, " 'you've gone through hell . . . all for nothin'.' " But the reader knows differently. Adam's escape into the desert, his years of searching, doubt, and purgation, his misguided attempts to rescue people, his desires to reconcile nature and God, and his spiritual lessons received under a throbbing sun, have made him a different man.

For Adam Larey—for Zane Grey—survival of the desert means the prospect of a meaningful life. Only through Adam's guilt and shame can he eventually become receptive to wisdom and atonement. The comfortable, unexamined life only leads to the refrigeration and paralysis of the soul; only through the wasteland is the spirit opened, vexed, challenged, renewed, and uplifted.

14

Apogee

Zane Grey and his family began the new decade of the 1920s on an auspicious note. After having lived at Lackawaxen for over fifteen years, they endured an unsettling move to California and spent a disruptive two-year interlude in temporary homes. In 1920 the Greys moved into a large, three-story Spanish-style house situated on five acres on Mariposa Street in Altadena. Surrounded by fan palms, spruces, and rose gardens, the house was soon festooned with Grey's hunting mementos, Navaho rugs, and Southwestern souvenirs.[1]

Grey soon established a routine that he kept for the eighteen years he spent there. Rising between six and seven in the morning, he breakfasted on pancakes, cereal, ham, and sausage. He then walked a mile and a half to the post office, enjoying his exercise as much as he did opening the day's mail. After returning home he usually talked with a fishing expert about tackle, making recommendations and preparations for the next angling adventure. Fishing tackle manufacturers frequently asked Grey for his endorsement of new products. He could talk about fishing endlessly, particularly with someone who shared his love of the sport.

Inevitably, however, Grey turned to his writing duties, which he performed on a rugged lapboard that rested on the arms of a comfortable Morris chair. He tucked a pillow behind him and went to work. At times he attacked his writing, producing one hundred thousand words in a single month. Other times, nettled by business distractions, his movie deals, or his children, he doodled in the margins of the paper, unable to force feeling into his prose. For the most part, Grey was a binge writer, and once in the throes of creation, he proceeded unimpeded, except to eat and sleep. When researching a new novel, he obtained everything on the subject. Books, magazines, and brochures teetered on the tables in his room. Sometimes, as with the manuscript of *The Desert of Wheat,* he stapled current newspaper clippings to the margins of the text. His notebooks, brimming with firsthand observations, were also nearby. Surrounded by Southwestern memorabilia, from lampshades decorated with Navaho motifs to trasteros draped in Apache buckskins, he entered his own private world.

Man of the Forest, published by Harper's in 1920 and laden with Darwinian thinking, climbed to the top of the best-seller list.

Grey did the original research with Al Doyle in the Tonto Basin of Arizona in 1915. The actual writing of the novel was completed between 1916 and 1917 (*Country Gentleman* began publishing the serialization October 20, 1917). *Man of the Forest* has a simple, even trivial, plot with influences from Grey's beloved Robinson Crusoe. It tells the story of Milt Dale, an uncouth misfit living in the White Mountains of Arizona, who loathes people and bonds to animals instead. Psychologically "marooned," Dale finds a woman in the village who is in *real* trouble. Removing Helen Rayner to his remote cabin in the mountains, he soon falls in love with her and through their relationship begins a slow connection to humanity. Along the way, Grey serves up generous portions of Darwin, Spencer, and ideas of his own; nature

A Grey family portrait in the yard at Altadena, California, c. 1930. Grey *(seated, right)* and Dolly *(standing, second from left)* had three children: Romer and Betty *(standing, right)* and Loren *(seated, middle)*. *Courtesy of the G. M. Farley Collection, Hagerstown, Maryland*

and God; self-preservation; homespun versus organized religion; and survival of the fittest. Again a character rescues to be rescued, and love blossoms in the inscrutable world of nature and time. Man's simple possession is love, admits Grey, a bulwark against the cruelties of life: "If you're quick to see, you'll learn that the nature here in the wilds is the same as that of men—trees fight to live—birds fight—animals fight—men fight. They all live off one another."[2]

The Mogollon Rim and Tonto Basin, northeast of Phoenix, provided Grey with settings for numerous ensuing novels.[3] When *Man of the Forest* was hitting the best-seller lists, Grey returned to these areas in Arizona. He had been there in the autumn of 1918 with R.C. and several companions, and then again in fall 1919 with R.C. and his wife, Al Doyle, Doyle's son Lee, Elma Swartz and friend, and the Haughts. The Haughts had arrived in the basin in 1897, ten years after the famous

Pleasant Valley feud erupted between the Tewksburys and the Grahams. On his 1920 expedition, Grey was intrigued by the feud and wished to discover more, but was met with such conflicting information that he gave up the search in despair.[4] Despite this setback, Grey still found his affection for the region growing. He decided to build a cabin in the rim country on three acres owned by the Haughts. Although Grey had plans for a log cabin, the Haughts surprised him with their own ideas. A famous western author needed more than a humble shanty: the Haughts built for Grey a white, green-trimmed bungalow in a magnificent setting in the forest. The house proved perfect for hunting expeditions, informal gatherings, and, at times, for secluded writing.

Eventually that year Grey broke through the Pleasant Valley denizens' reluctance to reveal the truth of the Tewksbury-Graham feud. After delving into much research, Grey wrote *To the Last Man* (Harper's edition 1922), a novel loosely based on the conflict and one of the most violent of Grey tales. Caught in the crossfire of the feud, two lovers, one from each family, try to weather their parent's antagonism. The very private war drags on, with Grey doing an excellent job of analyzing the bitterness and savagery of hatred—a hatred that has its own peculiar life quite apart from the families involved.

Even though Grey's attempts at western dialogue are sometimes inaccurate and frequently even silly, he enjoyed, and excelled at, writing about gunfights and duels. The following passage from *To the Last Man* illustrates the extent of his reliance on a belief in the terse, vivid sentence:

> *"Don't anybody move!"*
> Like a steel whip this voice cut the silence. It belonged to Blue. Jean swiftly bent to put his eye to a crack in the door. Most of those visible seemed to have been frozen into unnatural positions. Jorth stood rather in front of his men, hatless and coatless, one arm outstretched, and his dark profile set toward a little man just inside the door. This man was Blue. Jean needed only one flashing look at Blue's face, at his leveled, quivering guns, to understand why he had chosen this trick.

"Who're—you?" demanded Jorth, in husky pants.

"Reckon I'm Isbel's right-hand man," came the biting reply. "Once tolerable well known in Texas. . . . *King Fisher!*"

The name must have been a guarantee of death. Jorth recognized this outlaw and realized his own fate. In the lamplight his face turned a pale greenish white. His outstretched hand began to quiver down.

Blue's left gun seemed to leap up and flash red and explode. Several heavy reports merged almost as one. Jorth's arm jerked limply, flinging his gun. And his body sagged in the middle. His hands fluttered like crippled wings and found their way to his abdomen. His death-pale face never changed its set look nor position toward Blue. But his gasping utterance was one of horrible mortal fury and terror. Then he began to sway, still with that strange, rigid set of his face toward his slayer, until he fell. (p. 215)

In November 1921 Al Doyle died of cancer. Grey was at his bedside in Flagstaff during his last days. Doyle, who had accompanied Grey on so many adventures in Utah and Arizona, was one of Grey's significant mentors. With Old Muddy, Dolly Grey, Buffalo Jones, Jim Emmett, John and Louisa Wetherill, Al Doyle was a vital friend. He influenced Grey during the decade 1910–1919, a decade in which Grey matured as a person and writer, and a decade in which he vaulted into the limelight.

Doyle's passing represented the death of an era. Sadly, the Old West was vanishing. Buffalo Jones had died in 1916; now Doyle was gone. Grey was approaching fifty years of age. Black Fords honked down the streets of Flagstaff where horses and mules used to be tethered. Tourists were infiltrating the primitive tracts of land. Hotels were going up. Railroads were spreading tracks into the wasteland. The great empty spaces were melting away like snowflakes in the sun.

Other events in 1921 helped boost Grey's spirits. In March Grey was feted by his hometown of Zanesville, Ohio. Grey had sent a copy of *Betty Zane* in 1903 to the Zanesville paper, and in 1905 he had mailed his marriage announcement clipped from a New York newspaper.

Other than spotty correspondence, his association with Zanesville had been minimal.

But Zanesville had not forgotten him. The whole town rallied to show him its pride. The movie version of *The Desert of Wheat* had just been released, and Grey watched it with a cheering crowd jammed into Weller Theater. After the film, Grey got up on stage and was so overcome with emotion and embarrassment that he sputtered through his speech.[5]

Afterwards Grey avoided the crowds and spent his time visiting his old haunts. He returned to his boyhood home on Convers Avenue and behind the house located the cave where he had written his first story, "Jim of the Cave." Grey recalled the poignant, painful moment when his father tore up his manuscript and humiliated him for his writing effort—an event that shadowed Grey all his life.

His return was bittersweet, filled with vivid memories of childhood and tinged with the pathos of the present. "All was changed," he reflected grimly. The "palace" that he had grown up in was in fact "plain, small, drab [in] appearance."[6] The old fishing grounds were now a summer resort. The crumbling plank bridge had disappeared and now an iron bridge spanned the river. At Dillon's Falls he relived the barefoot summer moments. Old Muddy Miser was dead; only the falls could speak for him. He had carried the memory of this lush retreat around with him for over thirty years. He also could remember Muddy's words to him: "Surely someday somebody will venture to go after [the] giant fish. Perhaps you will be the one. I wish I could live to have you tell me about them . . ."

Sad and strangely elated, filled with "awe, wonder and gratitude," Grey left Zanesville after a few days and returned to California. The tender emotions raised by his homecoming remained with him for several years.

Several weeks after Al Doyle's death in November 1921, Grey was in Altadena rewriting a novel that was to become *The Day of the Beast*. Originally titled *Lethe,* this was the manuscript that Grey had started in 1905, two years after the publication of his first novel. Worked and reworked over the next fifteen years or so, it lay in mothballs until after the World War. Ostensibly it was that conflict and its aftermath that spurred Grey to resurrect it.

By the end of the war and into the new decade, Grey was fed up with the direction of modern life. He disliked "all the freedom of the young people, the jazz and dance and ridicule, and their rotten sensual stuff . . . the effect has been to depress and sadden and hurt me terribly."[7] Moreover, he hated to see returning veterans treated with indifference. The twenties were just beginning to roar, and Grey did not like what he heard. Being a socially conscious writer, he thought that dusting off and updating *Lethe* might swing America back to Grey's conservative ideals. He titled his novel *The Shores of Lethe,* but *Country Gentleman* published it as *The Day of the Beast,* beginning April 1, 1922.[8]

The Day of the Beast is one of only two novels by Grey written after 1918 that depart from western themes (the other being *The Reef Girl* [1939, not published until 1977], about Tahiti and the South Pacific), and is at best a poor, clumsy vehicle for his social protest. Dolly tried to warn him when she read it. "It will hurt you with some of your readers," she wrote him, "and you will get a lot of protestations."[9] No one, not even Dolly, could sway him, however. An aroused Grey, like an aroused lion, was simply unstoppable. When Harper's published it the same year, sales plummeted to an abysmal thirty thousand copies.

The Day of the Beast describes the return from war-ravaged Europe of Daren Lane, whose injuries include a bayonet hole in his back and a wounded leg. Lane, however, returns wearing a Croix de Guerre, awarded him by the French government for bravery in battle. Grey acerbically explains that the Americans had failed to report Lane's exploits, and hence, the wounded hero lacks an American medal for his heroism. Daren Lane's Croix de Guerre gets more attention than he does, one of the many instances in which Grey condemns America's treatment of war veterans.

To add to his shock in battle, Lane returns to an America whose moral fiber—particularly reflected in women's behavior—is fraying at the seams. Lane's aghast reaction to women's rouged cheeks and knee-length skirts may seem terribly old-fashioned, and Grey's references to Germans as the "barbaric, simian hun" may startle the modern reader who has forgotten the Great War, but these features form the bitter nucleus of this most unusual Grey novel. The new dancing, the lack of morals, and the rise of the brazen woman offend Lane—and Grey—and after that there is not much story to tell. Grey fears the coming of a liberal morality just about as much as the onset of another world war. Not having the West to flesh out his opinions, the novel struggles along without Grey's customary locales to give it a convincing background.

In *The Day of the Beast* Grey wished to prove to his critics, his readers, and himself that he could write a novel without a western setting. He desperately wanted to be a writer of the respectable, "philosophical" novel, in addition to being a writer of westerns. Unfortunately, this foray beyond the western novel was neither a critical nor a popular success.

While *Country Gentleman* serialized *The Day of the Beast* through April 1922, Grey began the background work for what he called his "Indian novel"—*The Vanishing American.* He revisited the areas that comprised his spiritual roost: the Painted Desert, Black Mesa, Kayenta, Monument Valley, and the Rainbow Bridge, making copious notes and talking to people on the Navaho reservation. His concentration was at fever pitch on this trip, perhaps because he was convinced that he was beginning the novel that he would be remembered by. He chatted with Navaho leaders, missionaries, traders, and government agents. If the modern morality and the world war hurt and depressed him, the emotional state of the Native American spurred him to action. But this time, the Indian's story unfolded on his turf, in a region close to his heart. Grey's affinity with the Southwest landscape is evident in the opening passage of the novel:

> At sunrise Nophaie drove his flock of sheep and goats out upon the sage slopes of the desert. The April air was cold and keen, fragrant with the dry tang of the uplands. Taddy and Tinny, his shepherd dogs, had wary eye and warning bark for the careless stragglers of the

flock. Gray gaunt forms of wolf and tawny shape of wild cat moved like shadows through the sage.

Nophaie faced the east, where, over a great rugged wall of stone, the sky grew from rose to gold, and a spendor of light seemed about to break upon the world. Nophaie's instinct was to stand a moment, watching and waiting without thought. The door of each hogan of this people opened to the rising sun. They worshiped the sun, the elements, all in nature.

Motionless he stood, an Indian lad of seven years, slim and tall, with this dark face turned to the east, his dark eyes fixed solemnly upon that quarter whence light and warmth always came. One thin brown hand held a blanket round his shoulders, and the other clasped his bow and arrows.

While he gazed a wondrous change came over the desert. The upstanding gloomy wall of rock far to the fore suddenly burned with a line of flame; and from that height down upon the gray lowlands shone the light of the risen sun. For Nophaie sunrise was a beginning —a fulfillment of promise—an answer to prayer. (p. 1)

After returning to California, Grey burrowed into writing *The Vanishing American.* He began the one-hundred-thousand-word-plus manuscript in early May and was finished by mid-June.[10] He remarked that he finished the novel free of depression—"an unprecedented record." This means that Grey traveled, researched, and wrote the draft and final manuscript of a great novel within a period of less than three months—an enormous feat and a testament to his energy and discipline as a writer.

Grey sold the serial rights of *The Vanishing American* to the *Ladies' Home Journal* (beginning November 1922); the novel, however, was not published by Harper's until 1925. Because it belongs to a separate phase of Grey's development, it will be discussed in the next chapter.

Between 1922 and 1924 Grey continued his frantic schedule of taking fishing trips (to Long Key, Oregon, Avalon, and Colorado, among other spots), writing books and articles, raising a family, monitoring scripts for Paramount Pictures, and keeping up with his favorite authors. When he was not working or fishing, he became nervous and irritable. In 1923 alone he published two novels, *Wanderer of the Wasteland* and the novelette *Tappan's Burro,* plus ten articles for periodicals ranging from *Country Gentleman* to *Boy's Life* and the *Izaak Walton Monthly.*

Just before Harper's published *Wanderer,* Grey received a request from the editors to shorten the text by three thousand words, which prompted Grey to fire back: "What do you suppose Conrad would say to such a proposition, or Tarkington?"[11] Grey eventually gave in, pruning some descriptions. He still maintained that it was his best novel to date.

With *Wanderer* being published the same year as *Tappan's Burro,* Grey achieved something of a coup: two great books appeared in the same year. Not since 1919, when *The Desert of Wheat* and *Tales of Fishes* were published, could Grey lay claim to such a feat. And yet *Tappan's Burro,* because of its simplicity and understatement, seemed an unlikely candidate for greatness among Grey's titles.

Published in *Ladies' Home Journal* in summer 1923 (Harper's clothbound edition followed shortly thereafter), *Tappan's Burro* is set in California's Mojave desert, Grey doing most of the background work while researching *Wanderer* in early 1919. Shorter than most of Grey's novels (and this is its strength), the novelette pays homage to the lowly but lovable burro, who follows without too many protests the prospectors and nomads of the desert.

In a tightly focused story Grey probes the relationship of the prospector Tappan and his durable animal friend, Jenet, in the white desert of Death Valley and later in the Superstition Mountains of Arizona. In several instances, Tappan saves Jenet, and Jenet returns the favor. Tappan moils for gold, sometimes abandoning the burro. But Jenet waits patiently for his return, knowing at some level that the miner's foolhardiness will pass. In a beautifully rendered sequence, Grey describes winter descending on the Arizona mountains. Jenet could plod through the desert, but is unable to walk through the snow.

Tappan won't leave her. Placing the burro in a folded tarp, Tappan drags her across the snow. Tappan is exhausted and hungry, but he perseveres through the forest. Finally reaching safety, Tappan frees Jenet on dry ground. Tappan falls peacefully to sleep—never to awaken.

Guilt over his treatment of his burro drives Tappan to perform his last-minute heroic act. The relationship of man and animal in their shared moments of helplessness and dependency is tenderly drawn and realistically rendered. Grey gives this relationship the equality that is missing from his romantic ones. The "dumb" burro becomes as important in the desert as any "intelligent" man, and in its own way is capable of greater sacrifice, bravery, and knowledge that its human counterpart.

Grey was pleased with *Tappan's Burro*. It helped balance his experiences hunting and exploiting animals and gave his work a sensitive dimension not seen since *Wildfire* in 1917. The *Journal's* editors liked it too, paying Grey the highest price it had ever offered a writer.[12]

By the mid 1920s, after nearly twenty years of reading critics' barbs, slights, attacks, gouges, and outright derision, Grey had simply had enough. It was customary for him after finishing a novel to swear not to read the critics' reviews of it. Usually he broke this promise to himself, perhaps hoping for a rave criticism among the negative ones. Moreover, he took personally the reviews of his work, which only exacerbated his pain and anger and self-doubt.

Perhaps the final straw came in 1923, when *Wanderer of the Wasteland*, the novel that Grey said that he would "stand or fall on," was panned by influential *New York Tribune* critic Burton Rascoe. Rascoe accused Grey's character Adam Larey of being a meddler in other people's business and called Grey's "moral ideas . . . decidedly askew." Rascoe concluded with: "Do Mr. Grey's readers believe in the existence of such people as Mr. Grey depicts; do they accept the code of conduct implicit in Mr. Grey's novels?"[13]

Grey sat down and wrote a twenty-page treatise titled "My Answer to the Critics." Poised, restrained but full of venom, he wrote out methodically what he had tried to accomplish in his work and how the critics had misjudged his efforts. He had desired to write great literature, on a level with Stevenson, Hugo, and Defoe and to reach a "great audience. I chose to win that through romance, adventure, and love of the wild and beautiful nature. The West appealed tremendously to my imagination. I recognized it as one of the greatest fields for an American novelist. . . . I hoped and prayed that the critics would judge me not from the result but from the nature of my effort."

Clearly, this was an unrealistic expectation on Grey's part. But because he believed so strongly in toil and the work ethic he thought his views were justified and defensible.

Of a fellow Ohioan, Sherwood Anderson, he concluded: "Mr. Anderson may be a great writer. But, if so, why did he not use his gifts toward the betterment of the world? Why not write of the struggle of men and women toward the light . . . ? He is a destroyer, not a builder."[14]

Grey also tried to defend his treatment of western themes and character types by claiming that he had known numerous cowboys like Venters in *Riders of the Purple Sage* and met women as "sweet and innocent and ignorant of life" as Fay Larkin in *The Rainbow Trail*. He went on: "Western people know I am absolutely true to the setting of my romances." He concluded with a plea directly to the critics, to ask the people who read his books—"your janitor, your plumber . . . the fireman and engineer."[15] These are the ones, thought Grey, who should be commenting objectively on his work. Of the critics themselves, he said simply: "They do not *know.*"

Grey at first wished to publish his treatise, but Dolly persuaded him not to. Its publication would only have aggravated matters between Grey and his critics, and would have served to reveal Grey's many insecurities in a public forum. Afterwards, Grey was less bothered by criticism of his work. He wrote Dolly in 1923: "I have begun to write again. Another romance! Where do I find these romances? That query has been promulgated by critics and reviewers who have been west. I see these romances, and I believe them. Somewhere, sometime, they happen."[16]

Returning to his Morris chair and the redoubtable lapboard astride it, Grey resumed being the most successful and popular author of his age.

Pilgrim at Nonnezoshe

Grey gave four of his novels titles that contain the words "last" or "vanishing." Like James Fenimore Cooper he was fascinated by the singularity and uniqueness of a person, animal, or thing poised on the brink of departing the world. *The Vanishing American* may be Grey's most important work, and it certainly is the vehicle that best conveys his intense outrage of the treatment of Navahos and Native Americans. It also is the benchmark of Grey's own departure from serious fiction. If the Indians in *The Vanishing American* face extinction, so do Zane Grey's noble convictions about and his passionate enthusiasm for the culture of the American West.

Several factors brought about the Navaho's plight. Ironically, the land that nourished Grey spiritually—northern Arizona and southern Utah—provided the resident Navahos a sunbaked, barren soil to support their attempts to grow crops and raise animals. One reservation Indian agent remarked that the land was "about as valuable for stock grazing as that many acres of blue sky." The climate also was punishing. Drought, frost, and grasshopper plagues were common. Between 1870 and 1902, records reveal the yearly cycle of hopelessness and frustration:

> 1870: Crops insufficient. Bad Navahos will steal, good ones starve; 1871: No crops; 1873: Grain gone by December—then six months without food; 1876: Wheat destroyed by grasshoppers; 1879: Drought; 1880: Drought; 1881: Drought, then floods; 1882: Good crop, but yearly frost spoiled much; 1893: Drought, people starving; 1894: Bad crops and price of wool down . . . Help needed; 1895: Great suffering . . . animals killed for food; 1900: Poor crops; 1901: Poor crops, rations used; 1902: Same . . . Rations issued winter and spring.[1]

The Navahos (called Nopahs by Grey in the novel) came to the reservation in the Four Corners area in 1869, after a period of imprisonment in New Mexico. They were skilled weavers and silversmiths, and these trades saw the Navahos through the harsh times on the reservation. To foster a sense of administration, Washington sent an Indian agent to the reservation. These men had little or no knowledge of Navaho culture; generally they accepted political favors and padded their $1200 yearly salary with bribes and slush money. The average stay for an agent from the East was one to two years at the most. Between 1869 and 1899, the reservation saw fifteen agents come and go. Generally, their mission was to maintain control, to distribute ration shipments, and to decide on special favors.[2]

The missionaries sent out to the reservation were no better equipped. The government established compulsory education for Navahos before their return to the reservation in 1869. Ill-prepared but passionate missionary educators soon made their way to the Navaho towns, ready to dispense their biblical knowledge with little regard for the Indians' religious system. However, attendance was erratic. Navaho children, used to the open air and their native ceremonies, stayed away from schoolhouses in droves. Gradually as peace between whites and Native Americans increased, Navaho parents and children grew to accept the idea of an Anglo education. But for the Indian agent, as well as the missionary, the bottom line was power—power over the land, power over a "heathen" people, and power over minds and emotions.[3]

The Navaho struggle to preserve their identity, culture, and religion amid an often corrupt white administration ignited Grey's sympathy for the downtrodden. Not since World War I had events galvanized his emotions. He sped through the writing of *The Vanishing American* in May and June of 1922.

When it was serialized by *Ladies' Home Journal* in November, religious groups were up in arms over Grey's treatment of missionaries in the novel. Among other derogatory things, Grey wrote that "the good missionary's life is a martyrdom, his fight against the parasitical forces noble as it is futile, and his task of transforming the Indian's religion of nature to the white man's creed one well nigh impossible."[4] Grey believed that altering the Navahos' religious system would quickly lead to their extinction. Grey was adamant on this point. However, his views on missionaries and their zeal to convert other people point to a major contradiction in Grey's moral thinking. On one hand, he seems to support his heroes who force their wills on others; on the other he can't stand the thought of a religious group forcing its ideas on the Navahos.

In August 1923, *Ladies' Home Journal* editor Burton Carrie wrote Harper's editor William Briggs to advise him that the controversy should not affect book sales. Harper's was due to publish *The Vanishing American,* but the editors were worried of a backlash by conservative Christian groups. The delay angered Grey.[5] During this time, Harper's suggested several structural changes in the novel; Grey complied. After the third revision of the manuscript, he wrote Briggs at Harper's: "I have studied the Navaho Indians for twelve years. I know their wrongs. The missionaries sent out there are almost everyone mean, vicious, weak, immoral, useless men. . . . My purpose was to expose this terrible condition—to help the great public to understand the Indians' wrongs." Grey added that he thought that religious groups wouldn't read his books anyway. "If I offended them no matter. If it aroused a controversy—well and good . . . eventually it is going to be believed. The truth always comes out."[6]

For Grey, the white man's lifelong struggle is to achieve the harmony with nature and God that the American Indian is blessed with from birth. In *The Vanishing American,* however, the young Indian Nophaie must relearn this relationship, after a long sojourn in the eastern United States. This is the essential conflict in the novel, as the earth child Nophaie returns to the corrupt, often vicious world of the reservation, hoping to balance his love for a white woman with his rediscovery of his Indian heritage. As the novel unfolds, it is a precarious balance at best.

"Rescued" by well-meaning Anglo tourists at age seven, Nophaie is reared in the East and attends college, where he distinguishes himself as a superb athlete. He meets Marian Warner, a white coed who becomes his college sweetheart. At this point the built-in conflicts are enough for one novel, but Grey complicates things further. Nophaie and Marian, on separate journeys, travel to Arizona, Nophaie to return to his culture and Marian to see the place of Nophaie's upbringing. They try to renew their love on the Nopah reservation, but there are initial problems. Nophaie's view of God unsettles Marian, challenging her Christian beliefs. On the reservation he knows that he cannot adopt the culture of white civilization, lifestyles, or religion. Nature has claimed him; his freedom becomes paramount to any love he could experience with a white woman. Gradually the star-crossed love between Nophaie and Marian becomes hopelessly thwarted by their different cultural backgrounds and entrenched viewpoints.

Fueling this separation are the conditions on the Nopah reservation. It is run by the manipulative, Machiavellian, and ruthless missionary named Morgan and the equally treacherous agent, Blucher, whom Grey characterizes as having "the German look." Together, they direct the reservation with chilling control and with absolutely no regard for the Nopah's welfare. Blucher longs for the Great War in Europe to involve America, thereby reducing scrutiny of his handling of the reservation. Morgan spouts the Gospel while trying to seduce young Indian women. The two are devious and disgusting, possessing that macho depravity that characterizes so many administrators in remote outposts.

Morgan's and Blucher's actions soon involve Nophaie, who tries to stand up for the sanctity of the Nopah's character and religion. At one point Nophaie beats the two men to bloody pulps. "'I ought to kick you too,'" says Nophaie. "'But I have a white man's education.'" Driven by fear, Nophaie heads for the sanctuary of the canyons north of Kaidab, and there slowly begins to connect with nature. Only news of the U.S. going to war with Germany brings him from his hideout. He returns to Kaidab, rallies his Indian brothers for war, and is shipped to the front in France. Returning home in 1918 a decorated soldier, he falls gravely ill with the influenza that is sweeping the reservation.[7] "'I'm in a strange mood,'" he tells Marian; "'I want solitude. And somehow Naza [Nonnezoshe] calls. There's light for me in those silent canyons.'"

Marian replies: "'Oh, if you could only find peace!'"

And so begins Nophaie's pilgrimage to Naza, the Rainbow Bridge, in search of the final spiritual connection which brings with it wisdom and serenity. He goes alone. "He meant not to exchange one word with a living soul while on this pilgrimage." He rides, as Grey had done, through the desert of death, the incarnation of all the Native American tribes fading slowly into the desert sun. "'The Indian's deeds are done,'" mutters Nophaie. "'Those of him who survive the disease and drink and poverty forced upon him must inevitably be absorbed by the race that has destroyed him. Red blood into white!'" Extinction! Weary and ill, he plods on, his hatred of Morgan and Blucher dominating his spirit. Even Marian's love cannot overcome it.

He reaches Naza, Indian symbol of eternal nature and timelessness. "The world of man, race against race, the world of men and women, of strife and greed, of hate and lust, of injustice and sordidness . . . the rush and fever of the modern day with its jazz and license and drink and blindness—these were not here in the grand shadow of Naza."[8] Nophaie muses that "the white man had not yet made Naza an object of destructiveness." Like the luxuriant oasis of the free Indian's soul, Naza would remain untouched by time, war, hunger, poverty, and chaos. As long as it remained, so would the Indian's spirit. After this realization, Nophaie feels that the "tragic fate of the vanishing American . . . ceased to exist." Experiencing a kind of Gethsemane of the spirit, Nophaie is prepared for his death and transcendence, secure in the knowledge that his desert journey brings his life to completion. He faces his death calmly and with resignation, even when Marian cannot fully comprehend his victory. Dying, Nophaie whispers to Marian that " 'all is well,' " echoing Christ's transcendent words from the cross: "It is finished."

Grey wrote two endings to the novel. The first, which appeared in serial form, has Nophaie returning to Kaidab to marry Marian. *Ladies' Home Journal* readers were outraged that a white woman would marry an Indian. Hence, Grey rewrote the ending for the publication of Harper's hardcover edition. In this version, the one discussed here, Nophaie succumbs to the rigors of his journey and dies after returning from Naza. Because he preferred happy endings, Grey's original conception was the more comic-romantic version with Marian marrying Nophaie. The latter one, the tragic version, provides a different philosophical conclusion to Nophaie's struggle. But either ending is acceptable because the story is already over, if you will, before its final page.

Marian and Nophaie form the dualistic nature of Grey's personality. On one hand Marian is the dutiful, pragmatic, Anglo, easterner-come-West, who "chops wood and carries water." She is hard working and honest, intensely curious about the Indian's religion—the real Zane Grey. On the other hand Nophaie is the soul Grey would like to be: primitive, instinctual, desert-born, a scholar, athlete, distinguished war veteran—Native American to the core. The conflict arises when each personality seeks dominance and control over the other. Nophaie, of course, wins because for Grey spiritual certainty is paramount to mere physical existence. At the end of the book, the two personalities are reconciled because Nophaie finds at Naza both the Anglo and Indian God. The physical and spiritual, the Eastern and Western, the white and Indian selves are made harmonious. In Nophaie's and Marian's marriage, the races come together and flourish. In Nophaie's death, the two are already married in spirit, even though Grey suggests that Native Americans and whites have enormous cultural and religious gulfs between them. Therefore, with either ending there is a sense of completion, harmony, and victory.[9]

Similar to Helen Hunt Jackson's *Ramona* and Frank Waters's *The Man Who Killed the Deer*, Grey's *The Vanishing American* is the story of an outsider who transcends evil and oppression. It also is a damning indictment of the missionary system in America. In this respect it is in the vein of Upton Sinclair's *The Jungle*. (Grey even feared for his life on the reservation after publication of the book.) The novel also raises issues about the exploitation and mistreatment of Native Americans. The book's greatness, however, lies in how Grey wove these various strands into a capable novel. Supplying vivid description of the starkness and beauty of the reservation and creating characters who manipulate and struggle under its cloudless skies, Grey wrote a compelling human drama while dispensing some devastating social criticism.

16

Wanderer

Harper's publication of *The Vanishing American* in 1925 marked the culmination of Zane Grey's career as a literary artist. The novels following, with a few exceptions, are either inferior, contrived, rushed, sentimental, derivative, or simply corny. His great inspirational period, between 1910 and 1925, produced his ten best novels (in order of publication): *The Heritage of the Desert* (1910); *Riders of the Purple Sage* (1912); *The Light of Western Stars* (1914); *The Rainbow Trail* (1915); *Wildfire* (1917); *The U.P. Trail* (1918); *The Desert of Wheat* (1919); *Wanderer of the Wasteland* (1923); *Tappan's Burro* (1923); and *The Vanishing American* (1925). These are the novels on which Grey's literary reputation must rest. All he had to say about the West is in these books.[1]

There must be several reasons for his gradual decline. One is that Grey was simply out of gas, his themes pillaged, his character types exhausted, his spiritual journey in literature complete. Second, as the West grew more and more settled and commercial, he tended to with-

Grey deep-sea fishing in the early 1930s. He claimed that the role of the sea in shaping his identity equaled that of the desert. *Courtesy of the G. M. Farley Collection, Hagerstown, Maryland*

draw more from it. As time went on, he craved the primitive, unspoiled parts of the earth. Third, as he accumulated more income, he became enamored of fishing in and exploring the far-flung places, which took him away from the land he held so dear. The driving force in Grey's life was the need to escape—in writing, in fishing and wandering—any activity that took him out of reality and soothed his feelings. In the second half of the 1920s it is apparent that his large-scale fishing excursions were luring Grey from America, and that the money he needed to fund them was being generated by his writing. Zane Grey, the two-fisted Lassiter of *Riders of the Purple Sage* had, by 1925, become the barefoot Ishmael of the Seven Seas.

Grey first broke loose from the bonds of the North American continent in 1925, when he, R.C., Romer, and several others sailed from San Diego to the Galapagos Islands off Peru. These were the islands that Darwin had studied so carefully on the voyage of the *Beagle*. As a student of the scientist, Grey was pleased to be on the island on which Darwin had made his studies. The size and diversity of fish, however, impressed him more, whetting his appetite for even more distant angling adventures.

Late in the same year Grey and friend Captain Laurie Mitchell decided on a voyage to Tahiti and New Zealand. Sailing on board the *Royal Mail S.S. Makura* on December 30, they reached Papeete in early January 1926. Grey's romantic visions of Tahiti were quickly dashed, however, as he was greeted by unkempt beachcombers, shopkeepers, and areas of squalor and decay.

They proceeded on to New Zealand, where Grey was entranced by the unspoiled paradise. The Maoris of the island fascinated Grey, long a student of man's primitive past. Moreover, he even found tattered copies of his books in their villages.

In New Zealand and the South Pacific Grey found a verdant landscape that slowly seduced him. He returned there in 1927 and 1932, and to Tahiti in 1929. The early 1930s saw him mounting even larger-scale fishing excursions, hoping to match or outdo the previous ones.

Between 1926 and his death in 1939, Grey continued his novel-writing regimen. He also resumed his attempt to capture the entire western experience. He featured cowboys (*The Drift Fence*, 1923; *The Hash Knife Outfit*, 1933); gunmen (*Forlorn River*, 1927; *Nevada*, 1928); Native Americans (*Blue Feather*, 1961); and horses (*Wild Horse Mesa*, 1928;

Valley of Wild Horses, 1947). He discussed various historical events such as the Maxwell Land Grant in northern New Mexico (*Knights of the Range,* 1939), and the impact of the telegraph on the West (*Western Union,* 1939). And, too, his settings hopscotched around the region, from Idaho (*Thunder Mountain,* 1935) and Colorado (*Raiders of Spanish Peaks,* 1938), to Oregon (*Rogue River Feud,* 1948) and Texas (*West of the Pecos,* 1937). As he had done through 1917, he continued his exploration of all aspects of western life, turning out a novel—sometimes two or three—per year. His themes, which early in his career dwelled on Mormonism and Darwinism, on the effects of World War I, the decline of modern morality, and the mistreatment of Native Americans, soon passed into explorations of the cowboy and his world, of the death of the buffalo, and of life in the contemporary West. The fire of Grey's passion burned intensely in the early novels; it began to smolder and die out in the late 1920s and early 1930s.

Although his attraction to the South Pacific began to take hold in the 1920s, Grey had not totally abandoned his travels through the West. After his New Zealand voyage in 1926, he loaded his family into the car and headed to Phoenix. They toured the Tonto Basin and Salt Water Canyon. A year later Grey was back at his Tonto Basin cabin, where he found consolation and inspiration in the forested isolation, a sense of being one with the forest with which he endows the character Lucy in *Under the Tonto Rim* (1926):

> She found out, presently, that going into the forest was a source of comfort. When there seemed no comfort she went to the lonely solitude of trees and brush, of green coverts and fragrant wild dells, and always she was soothed, sustained. She could not understand why, but it was so. She began to prolong the hours spent in the woods, under a looming canyon wall, or beside a densely foliaged gorge from which floated up the drowsy murmur of stream. All that the wild forest land consisted of passed into her innermost being. She sensed that the very ground she trod was full of graves of races of human beings who had lived and fought there, suffered in their blindness and ignorance, loved and reared their young, and had grown old and died. No

Grey receiving congratulations on a world-record catch—a 1,036-pound tiger shark—in Sydney, Australia, in 1936. By 1930, Grey was as serious about fishing as writing. *Courtesy of the G. M. Farley Collection, Hagerstown, Maryland*

trace left! No more than autumn leaves! It seemed to be this lesson of nature that gradually came to her. Thereafter she went to the woods early in the mornings as well as the afternoon, and finally she had courage to go at night.

And it was at night she came to feel deepest. Darkness emphasized the mystery of the forest. Night birds and crickets, prowling coyotes with their haunting barks, the wind sad and low in the pines, the weird canopy of foliage overhead studded with stars of white fire—these taught her the littleness of her life and the tremendousness of the spirit from which she had sprung. She was part of the universe. The very fear she had of the blackness, the beasts, and the unknown told of her inheritance. She came at length to realize that this spell engendered by nature, if it could be grasped in its entirety and held, would make bearable all aches of heart and miseries of mind. Her contact with actual life covered twenty little years in a town, among many people; her instincts, the blood that beat at her temples, the longings of her bones, had been bred of a million years in the solitude and wild environment of the dim past. That was why the forest helped her.
(pp. 259–60)

From his Tonto Rim cabin, Grey viewed the growing commercialism around Flagstaff with concern.[2] Grey's final trip to his beloved desert country occurred in 1929, when he and a party of ten people motored through southern Utah and northern Arizona, eventually ending up in Flagstaff. In Flagstaff he hoped to scout film locations with Fox studios director R. E. Houck, and then rest at his Tonto cabin. Grey applied to the state game warden to hunt a menacing bear out of season.[3] Ultimately his request was denied, the case being sensationalized in the Arizona papers. Hurt and angry, Grey withdrew his interest in Arizona, and in 1930 he made his objections public by writing a Flagstaff newspaper and citing the reasons for leaving. One reason was the refusal to grant him a special resident license to hunt bears, and the publicity surrounding it. Grey also noted that tourism and other commercial ventures were ruining Arizona, and that he simply could not stand by and watch this happen.[4]

And so by the new decade of the 1930s, Zane Grey watched from the California shore as Arizona's once wild and remote landscape was overrun by tourists, speculators, and developers. Like the character of Slingerland in *The U.P. Trail*, he turned his back on a West that seemed to be forever "vanishing—vanishing—vanishing."

Approaching sixty years of age in 1931, Grey sailed to Fiji. He had slowed down somewhat, physically. He was a bit heftier (but not much) than in his Lackawaxen days, with a thick shock of white hair, but he still bore the passionate eyes and granite resolve of his youth. Just before another expedition, Grey invited fellow writer and fisherman Ernest Hemingway on a world cruise during which they could make a movie. Hemingway thought Grey was jealous of the former's fishing acumen and wished to exploit Hemingway's fame to boost his own.[5] As a result, the excursion never came about.

While Grey flitted about the world, Dolly Grey maintained her position as his major critic, champion of his effort, and chief architect of the business end of his writing. She had read and offered an opinion on virtually every word Grey ever wrote. Her knowledge of literature was extensive; her instinct for shaping the quality of Grey's early work was profound. In the 1920s she shrewdly and gradually raised the price of a Grey serial in *Country Gentleman* from $35,000 to $50,000. In *American* she bargained for and got $60,000, and at *Collier's* she engineered $80,000 per serialization.[6] By the 1920s Grey was splitting royalty checks with Dolly. Zane spent his share on fishing trips, land, ships, cabins, and so forth. Dolly ran the house and saved enough to fund two European vacations for herself.[7]

As Depression blues began to erode the countryside in the early 1930s, the serial market in major magazines nearly dried up. Publishers could no longer afford Grey's high prices and were forced to seek cheaper authors to serialize. Grey had three serials running in 1932; one in 1933; one in 1936. Hurt further as the Depression deepened, the serialization of Grey's books had by 1937 not only dipped but tobogganed. The halcyon days of the twenties, when he could have five or six serials running in a single year, were over.

His zeal for writing western romances, however, remained undimin-

Zane Grey in Australia, c. 1936. Grey stayed current with advances in fishing tackle. Here he is shown with deep-sea tackle. *Courtesy of the G. M. Farley Collection, Hagerstown, Maryland*

ished. Between trips to Australia in 1935 and fishing adventures in Oregon, Grey wrote quickly, intensely, and voluminously. He could still conjure up that sense of awe in face of the elemental struggle of man and beast against the forces of unyielding nature, in scenes he describes with unflagging gusto in *The Trail Driver* (1936):

> Spellbound, Brite gazed at the thrilling and frightful spectacle. A gigantic wave rose and swelled across the creek to crash over the opposite bank. In another moment the narrow strip of muddy water vanished, and in its place was a river of bristling horns, packed solid, twisting, bobbing under and up again, and sweeping down with the current. But for that current of deep water the stream bed would have been filled with cattle from bank to bank, and the mass of the herd would have plunged across over hundreds of dead bodies.
>
> In an incredibly short space the whole herd had rolled into the river, line after line taking the place of the beasts that were swept away in the current. From plunging pell-mell the cattle changed abruptly to

swimming pell-mell. And when the last line had gone overboard the front line, far down the stream, was wading out on the other side.

The change from sodden, wrestling crash to strange silence seemed as miraculous as the escape of the herd. Momentum and current forced the crazy animals across the river. Two hundred yards down all the opposite shelving shore was blotted out by cattle, and as hundreds waded out other hundreds took their places, so that there was no blocking of the on-sweeping tide of heads and horns.
(pp. 258–59)

In the 1930s Grey published fifteen western novels, as well as a score of articles and stories. Even after his death in 1939, Harper and Brothers had stockpiled enough Grey manuscripts that they could release them, one a year, through 1963. Although the later novels do not measure up to his earlier work, they are proof that Grey simply could not say enough about his adopted countryside.

His relationships with Hollywood studios continued to deteriorate in the 1930s. With the advent of sound pictures, studios pushed to remake numerous silent pictures. This haste, coupled with the need to make more films on movie lots rather than on location, began to erode Grey's longstanding commitment to authenticity of locale. Henry Hathaway, who directed many westerns of the thirties, shared Zane Grey's drive for accuracy. However, there were times in Depression-lean Hollywood that even Hathaway resorted to using location footage from earlier films.[8]

By the mid and late 1930s Hollywood's star system was well established. Once chided by Grey as Hollywood's downfall, the system created several name actors through associations with Grey's works. In 1930 and 1931 George O'Brien rose to prominence in Grey movies. Randolph Scott, who came west to restore his health, enjoyed early success in *The Heritage of the Desert* (1931) and *Sunset Pass* (1933). Both films were among the first sound pictures based on Grey's books. Paramount Pictures introduced Larry "Buster" Crabbe through three Grey properties: *Nevada* (1935), *Drift Fence* (1936), and *Desert Gold* (1936). Later John Wayne and Robert Mitchum acted in movies based on Grey's novels. Overall, from the silents through sound pictures, Hollywood (with a number of prominent directors, actors, and actresses) produced over one hundred feature films based on Zane Grey's books.[9]

శ్రా

In the l930s events in Grey's personal life began to cripple his resolve. Grey's older brother Ellsworth died in 1931. In 1934, R.C., his younger brother and fishing buddy, died of a heart attack, sending Grey into an emotional tailspin. His sister Ida, who had remained at Lackawaxen and then moved in with R.C., died of cancer in 1937. Fishing trips to Oregon and Washington and a major excursion to Australia in 1935 helped alleviate the pain of his losses. Other dark clouds gathered on the horizon. As the Depression dragged on, a violent new order, one even more evil than the one that threatened Europe in 1914, was gaining momentum in Germany. His self-imposed exile from Arizona and his worries about the economy only increased his anxiety and isolation.

In 1937, while fishing for steelhead in the North Umpqua River in Oregon, Grey collapsed from a heart attack and stroke. Reducing his schedule, he recovered through the next year at Altadena. On October 23, 1939, at 67 years of age, he was exercising on his porch when he suffered another, this time fatal, attack. He died shortly thereafter.

Millions of readers, even critics, mourned his passing.

17 🐎

A Summing-Up

Zane Grey's literary career spanned four decades. However, if we include the entire range of the years in which his books were initially published, the length of time reaches seven decades. Grey's prolific career seems even more remarkable when we consider his other roles: world-class fisherman and advisor to fishermen, explorer, sailor, husband, and father. Everything considered, he was an inexhaustible human spirit.

For the sake of analysis, Grey's extensive career can be divided into four major periods: the first (1903–1907) includes the three novels of the Ohio River trilogy—*Betty Zane, The Spirit of the Border,* and *The Last Trail.* The second (1908–1925) is Grey's zenith, and includes the novels *Riders of the Purple Sage, The U.P. Trail, The Vanishing American,* etc. The third phase (1926–1939) marks the period of Grey's decline, and features such works as *Nevada, The Drift Fence,* and *Western Union.* The fourth period (after his death in 1939) includes the last novels published posthumously at yearly intervals by Harper and

Brothers. This final phase contains only a handful of notable titles, among them *Blue Feather and Other Stories,* and *The Wilderness Trek.*

Instead of being revered as one of the West's serious novelists, Grey will probably be remembered as one of its chief folklorists. His secure place as a creator of myth is perhaps best understood by comparing him with another writer of the twentieth century, his contemporary, Robert Service. Service is known as the "bard of the Yukon." Although his name will never be mentioned in the same breath as T. S. Eliot, Ezra Pound, or Robert Frost, he will continue to delight readers with his stirring verses about Alaska and the Yukon.

Service was born in England in 1874, two years after Grey. With an avowed intent to become a cowboy, Service emigrated to Canada in 1896. Several years later, he took a job as a bank clerk in Whitehorse in the Yukon territory. It was the tail-end of the Klondike Gold Rush. During the long winter months, Service began to capture in verse what remained of "the trail of '98." Writing during the early 1900s, Service began to amass a body of poetry that gained him popular success and critical praise, including such favorites as "The Shooting of Dan Mc-Grew," "The Cremation of Sam McGee," "The Ballad of Blasphemous Bill," and "Clancy of the Royal Mounted Police." The Yukon had found its spokesman. By 1912 he was world famous. Today, in Alaska and the Yukon his name is mentioned with reverence. In popularity and book sales, he surpasses Jack London and Rex Beach, two authors who examined the more serious aspects of the Klondike Gold Rush.

What is true of Robert Service is true of Zane Grey. Service's name will be forever associated with the North not because he created necessarily a realistic account of its history, but because he developed an elaborate folklore about it. Grey did the same for the American West. By using romance and myth, Grey created larger-than-life heroes against a stark, spectacular landscape. His direct influence in the genre affected writers such as Max Brand, Ernest Haycox, Louis L'Amour, George G. Gilman, Tabor Evans, and Jake Logan.

In addition to his literary career, Grey also made remarkable inroads in the Hollywood western. During the 1920s and 1930s, Grey

Grey at his desk revising a manuscript, c. 1938—about a year before his death. Grey was a perfectionist as a writer, frequently rewriting key parts of a draft several times before sending it on to Dolly to be typed. *Courtesy of the G. M. Farley Collection, Hagerstown, Maryland*

was the guiding spirit of the popular B western. Actors like Randolph Scott came to Hollywood and created their careers starring in Zane Grey films. The Grey name associated with any movie was bound to give it wider viewership and higher revenues at the box office.

After Grey's death, the popularity of radio competed with the silver screen. To a great degree, radio targeted a younger audience, mainly children and teenagers. Even though Zane Grey was not a major force in radio of the 1940s, his themes of hard work, integrity, and hero worship continued to resonate in shows like *Tom Mix* and *The Lone Ranger*. Later in the 1940s, adult-oriented programs such as *Gunsmoke* presented a more mature view of the Old West.

In the 1950s the popular western virtually stampeded through American culture. On one hand, the cinema explored fresh trends in the western, helping to diversify the careers of directors like George Stevens and Fred Zinnemann and of actors like James Stewart, Alan Ladd, and Richard Widmark. Moreover, television produced a host of new western programs, including *Death Valley Days, Wagon Train, Sky King,* and *The Zane Grey Theater,* the latter helping to bring the Grey legend to a new generation of fans. But whether it was historical or modern, light-hearted or dramatic, the television western dominated family viewing throughout the decade. At one point in the fifties, twenty-four westerns ran in prime time each week.

In the 1990s, after several decades of western movies featuring anti-heroes and angst-ridden misfits, Grey's work appears to be on the verge of a minor renaissance. In early 1996, Grey's masterpiece, *Riders of the Purple Sage,* once again rode boldly onto the screen. Produced by Ted Turner Productions, this made-for-cable movie reinforced the idea that our nostalgia for the romantic west is perennially seductive. Directed with skill by Charles Haid, the 1996 version of *Riders of the Purple Sage* is a sincere adaptation of the original novel and is certainly a brilliant counterpoint to the flawed 1920s silent version. Although the Mormon influence is again downplayed, Haid understands Grey's affinity with the land. Haid accentuates in each frame the elemental and sculptural qualities of the red rock country of southeast Utah. Added to the strengths of the directing are Oscar-winner Ed Harris's portrayal of Lassiter and Amy Madigan's depiction of the defiant Jane Withersteen. Harris digs deep into the heroic male role, and Madigan is brilliantly cast to stand up to his dominating personality. For these reasons, Turner and Haid's collaboration is far and away the finest translation of Grey material for the screen.

❧

Although he essentially pioneered his own code of ethics in his novels (with help from James Fenimore Cooper), Grey had several literary mentors throughout his life: Nathaniel Hawthorne, Victor Hugo, Cooper, William Wordsworth, Owen Wister, Matthew Arnold, Joseph Conrad, W. H. Hudson, and Robert Louis Stevenson, among others.

Stevenson, in particular, occupied a special place in Grey's heart. For one thing, the Scots author had been west. Moreover, he had written about his western experiences in a remarkable little book titled *The Amateur Emigrant,* which detailed his journey from the British Isles to the plains and mountains of the American West in the summer of 1879. It is more than a simple journey, however: it is Stevenson's rite of passage to the New World. Grey loved it for that quality and referred to its pages over and over throughout his life. *The Amateur Emigrant* influenced *The U.P. Trail* and *Western Union,* as well as confirming for Grey that Stevenson was a comrade in arms.

Critic Heywood Broun's assertion that "the substance of any two Zane Grey books could be written upon the back of a postage stamp"[1] may be grossly stretching the point, but there is a nub of truth in the comment. At some point in his career, Grey knew it to be a valid, if cruelly overstated, criticism. However, he was not the only popular author of the twentieth century to lapse into a little formula writing. Mystery and adventure writers were as guilty of the charge as authors of westerns. But Grey may have been the most popular writer of the twentieth century to use the formula plot with such defiance and with such skill. If critics cringed at each new Zane Grey book in the hopper between 1930 and 1963, readers worldwide eagerly anticipated them.

In the final analysis Grey never matured as a novelist. John Updike once remarked that of "American novelists only Henry James continued in old age to advance his art; most, indeed, wrote their best novels first, or virtually first. Energy ebbs as we live; success breeds disillusion as surely as failure; the power of hope to generate action and vision lessens." As a result, this lack of maturity in Grey meant that he would never be ranked among the great writers of the twentieth century; however, it also meant that the West got its major writer of folklore and romance.

Zane Grey's strength lay in his ability to communicate on an emotional level the ruggedness and beauty of the American West. He was much more an instinctual than an intellectual artist. His journeys through desert and mountain terrain were nearly always fierce pilgrimages inside himself; his characters, beneath their hard-boiled exteriors, were groping for tender arms or lush sanctuaries.

Shaping this view was an angry, guilt-ridden author, who through his characters searched for some bright patches of green within the wasteland. At times he was embarrassed that he was a writer of westerns; other times he flaunted the fact. Intensely driven, he buried his emotions in travel, writing, fishing, or some tantalizing daydream. Isolation aggravated his blue moods; loneliness gnawed at him constantly. In his work he resolved a number of deep spiritual questions; in his private life, however, he stumbled toward a God that increasingly drifted away from him.

Some carped that Grey's work was not realistic. They said his gunmen and cowboys, his wild horses and buffalo hunters, his silent, tough drifters and independent women were hopelessly idealistic. There were other people, however, the majority, who claimed that if this wasn't how the Old West really was, it certainly was the way it *should* have been.

Notes

Chapter 1

1. Frank Gruber, *Zane Grey: A Biography* (New York: Signet, 1971), 4-10. See also Z.G. autobiography for Zane's impressions and feelings concerning Muddy Miser.
2. Gruber, 9.
3. Gruber, 20.
4. Gruber, 23-25.
5. Gruber, 24-26.
6. Ibid.
7. Z.G. autobiography. Also Carlton Jackson, *Zane Grey,* rev. ed. (Boston: G. K. Hall and Company, 1989), 21. Z.G. wrote his autobiography up through his college days. Among other revelations, it asserted that one of the reasons that the family moved to Columbus, Ohio, was that Z.G. had been found in a local brothel. Dr. Gray's problems, however, seem the more likely reason for the move.

Chapter 2

1. Gruber, 29.

2. Apparently Z.G. tried to sell some of these poems to journals in New York—without success. This would be his first attempt to sell something literary. G. M. Farley, letter to the author, June 7, 1992.

3. According to Frank Gruber, 34, as Grey approached the plate "a professor" in the stands shouted: "Grey, the honor of the University Of Pennsylvania rests with you." It is difficult to imagine in the clamor of a ninth inning how a player on the field could hear this clearly and distinctly.

Chapter 3

1. Grey scholar Carlton Jackson favors Z.G.'s choice of the British spelling, because it had its "value in American society." Letter to the author, January 15, 1992.

2. *Spirit of the Border,* 82.

3 Jackson, 50. The study of Darwin and Spencer was sweeping college classrooms during Z.G.'s day.

4. H. E. Bates, *Autobiography* (London: Jonathan Cape, 1972), 63.

5. Z.G. Diary, April 30, 1917.

6. Z.G. Diary, June 1, 1926.

7. Z.G. Diary, January 24, 1920.

Chapter 4

1. Folsom, "Precursors of the Western Novel," in *A Literary History of the American West,* ed. Thomas Lyon (Fort Worth: Texas Christian University Press, 1987), 143.

Chapter 5

1. Gruber, 45.

2. Gruber, 47.

3. Gruber, 46.

4. Z.G. Diary, August 8, 1910. Later Grey was influenced by British writer W. H. Hudson, author of *Green Mansions* (1904). According to G. M. Farley, in a letter to the author of June 22, 1992, Hudson's impact on Grey was profound and greater than previously thought. Given the idyllic, remote Grey settings, there may be a very strong connection between the authors.

5. Z.G. Diary, October 1, 1905.

6. Ibid.

7. Ibid.

8. Gruber, 49.

9. Gruber, 52.

10. Z.G., letter to Dolly Roth, September, 1905.

11. Dolly Roth, letter to Z.G, September 14, 1905.

Chapter 6

1. Dolly Grey, Diary, January 15, 1906.
2. Candace C. Kant, *Zane Grey's Arizona* (Flagstaff: Northland Publishing, 1984), 11.
3. Kant, 13.
4. Gruber, 65. The variant spelling of Emmett is Emett. Grey uses the former spelling in *The Last of the Plainsmen,* and that is the one I will use.
5. Kant, 15.
6. Gruber, 65.
7. Gruber, 66. Evidently, Z.G. thought *Betty Zane* was his best book, since he wished to make the best impression on Jones.
8. Gruber, 66.
9. Z.G., letter to Dolly Grey, March 27, 1907.
10. Z.G., letter to Dolly Grey, April 8, 1907. This statement is a little ironic, since Grey was to write fifty-six novels about the West.
11. Z.G., letter to Dolly Grey, April 12, 1907.
12. Kant, 15.
13. Gruber, 70.
14. Ibid.
15. *Last of the Plainsmen,* 18.
16. *Riders of the Purple Sage,* 13.
17. Z.G., "The Man Who Influenced Me Most."
18. Ibid.
19. Jackson, 31. Grey quoted this in "My Own Life," published in 1928 by Harper's. It can be viewed as his guiding credo in his uphill battle with the critics.
20. *Plainsmen,* 12.
21. Ibid., 26.
22. Ibid.
23. Preface, *To the Last Man.*

Chapter 7

1. Z.G. "My Own Life," 5.
2. Z.G. Letter to Daniel Murphy, undated.
3. Z.G. Letter to Daniel Rust, December 4, 1910, and January 2, 1911.
4. Ibid.
5. "Mormon Novels," in Lyon, ed., *A Literary History of the American West,* p. 850.

6. Gruber, 83.

7. For an excellent in-depth analysis of the hero's journey see Joseph Campbell's brilliant *Hero with a Thousand Faces,* Part 1, p. 49 (Princeton University Press, 1968); or for mythical patterns in Grey see Northrop Frye's "Archetypes in Literature" in *Fables of Identity: Studies in Poetic Mythology* (New York: Harcourt Brace, 1963).

8. Many readers claim this is a nearly impossible coincidence. However, Grey was aware of timing in romance writing, where events are more cyclical than linear. There is a sense of patterned time in romance. For example, it would be awkward in Chaucer's "Wife of Bath's Tale" for the knight to accomplish his task before his limit of days. In romance, the universe has a way of ordering itself to the deeds of the hero.

9. Z.G. autobiography, p.58.

10. With the character of Mescal, Grey begins a tradition of Indian characters who "bloom" in the desert soil.

Chapter 8

1. George Reiger, ed., *Zane Grey: Outdoorsman* (Englewood Cliffs, New Jersey: Prentice-Hall, 1972), 66.

2. Ibid.

3. Z.G. Letter to Daniel Murphy, June 2, no year.

4. Kant, 98.

5. *The Rainbow Trail,* 30.

6. See Arizona Census Figures.

7. Kant, 86.

8. Gruber, 104.

Chapter 9

1. Z.G. letter to Robert Davis, March 19, 1912.

2. Kant, 30.

3. Ibid.

4. Ibid., 109.

5. *Desert Gold,* 28.

6. See Douglas Allen, *N. C. Wyeth* (New York: Harcourt, 1968), 53.

7. The others were Blumenschein, Joseph Sharp, Oscar Berninghaus, Bert Phillips, and Irving Couse.

8. W. H. Hutchinson, *The World, the Work and the West of W. H. D. Koerner* (Norman: University of Oklahoma Press, 1978), 94.

9. Ibid., 119.

10. Ibid., 124.

Chapter 10

1. Reiger, 134.
2. Jackson, 115.
3. Grey, *Tales of Fishing Virgin Seas,* 95.
4. Gruber, 119.
5. *The Light of Western Stars,* 267.
6. Kant, 23. Apparently this was the first of numerous times that young women accompanied Grey on trips.
7. "Nonnezoshe" in *Recreation* (February 1915), p 70.
8. Ibid.
9. Ibid., 71.
10. Ibid., 76.
11. Ibid.
12. Ibid., 78.
13. Ibid.

Chapter 11

1. Gruber, 121.
2. Dolly Grey, Letter to Z.G., August 18, 1915.
3. Kant, 26.
4. Robert Easton, *Max Brand* (Norman: University of Oklahoma Press, 1970), 45–46.
5. Ibid., 49.
6. See Faust, *Notebooks and Poems*(unpublished manuscript), 24.
7. Easton, 68.
8. See Fred Erisman and Richard Etulain, eds., *Fifty Western Writers: A Bio-Bibliographical Guide* (Westport, Conn.: Greenwood Press, 1982), 184.
9. Ibid., 13.
10. Ibid., 16.
11. Ibid., 205.
12. Hutchinson, 144.
13. Z.G. Letter to Daniel Murphy, undated. Grey presumably means Theodore Roosevelt. Roosevelt typified the Grey hero. After the death of his mother and wife on the same day in 1884, Roosevelt traveled to a ranch in North Dakota that summer. Hoping to fill the deep emotional void with the western landscape, Roosevelt stayed on the ranch for two years, writing, observing, and punching cattle. Weak and bespectacled when he arrived, he was

known to the other ranchers as "the four-eyed dude." He soon became "educated" by the West, enduring the North Dakota winters and once decking a drunk rancher who got in his way. Roosevelt wrote of his experiences in *Ranch Life* (1888), which was illustrated by Frederic Remington. Roosevelt's transformation was a clear indication that the Grey protagonist was not only alive and well—but occupied the White House.

14. Z.G. Diary, April 7, 1917.

15. Z.G. Diary, April 5, 1917.

16. Jackson, 122.

17. Hutchinson, 141.

18. Ibid., 119.

19. Z.G. serialized seventeen novels with *Country Gentleman* between the years 1916 and 1934.

20. Gruber, 131.

Chapter 12

1. Lyon, ed., 266.

2. Ibid., 267.

3. Kant, 139.

4. For a fascinating look at Ford's development as a director of westerns see Andrew Sarris' *The John Ford Movie Mystery* (Bloomington, Ind.: Indiana University Press, 1971).

5. Gruber, 131.

6. Kant, 137.

7. Ibid., 138.

8. Z.G., Letter to Benjamin Hampton, May 1, 1919.

9. Kant, 138.

10. Ibid., 142.

11. Ibid., 145.

Chapter 13

1. *The U.P. Trail* was Grey's first western novel to use actual historical events as background.

2. Jackson, 54.

3. Gruber, 132.

4. Original manuscript, Library of Congress.

5. Z.G. Diary , December 29, 1918.

6. A binge alcoholic, Nielsen died mysteriously in Baja California in 1924.

7. For a complete record of this journey see Grey's "Death Valley," *Harper's,* April 22, 1920; or Gruber, 134–39.

8. His most recent desert novel was *The Rainbow Trail* (1915).

9. Z.G. Diary, January 19, 1919.

10. Ibid., February 19, 1919.

11. Ibid., March 29, 1919.

12. Ibid., April 27, 1919.

13. Ibid., May 22, 1919.

14. Ibid., May 29, 1919

15. Unless otherwise noted, all remaining quotes in this chapter are from *Wanderer of the Wasteland* (1923).

Chapter 14

1. Gruber, 159.

2. *Man of the Forest,* 126.

3. Z.G., not liking the pronunciation of "Mogollon," changed the name to "Tonto" Rim. Kant, 36.

4. Ibid., 35.

5. Gruber, 161.

6. Z.G. Diary, March 23, 1921.

7. Ibid., November 29, 1921.

8. Z.G. wanted to use the title *The Shores of Lethe*—Lethe being the mythological river that flowed through Hades and whose waters produced forgetfulness in people. However, *Country Gentleman's* preferred *The Day of the Beast,* a title perhaps suggested by Yeats's poem "The Second Coming": "And what rough beast its hour comes round at last slouches toward Bethlehem to be born."

9. Dolly Grey, Letter to Z.G., June 27, 1922.

10. Z.G. Diary, June 22, 1922. There is an ambiguity about the finishing date of the manuscript. He begins this entry by saying that he finished the novel on this date. However, later in the same entry he mentions that he completed the novel on June 8.

11. Z.G. Letter to Dolly Grey, July 6, 1922.

12. The following year (1924) Grey's production was simply phenomenal. It included the novel *Call of the Canyon* (another distraught veteran comes West for restoration book); plus two serials, *The Thundering Herd* and *Wild Horse Mesa;* several fishing articles, and the important feature article "What the Desert Means To Me"—*American* magazine, November 1924.

13. Burton Rascoe, *New York Tribune,* January 21, 1923.

14. Z.G., "My Answer to the Critics" (unpublished essay).

15. Ibid.

16. Z.G. Letter to Dolly Grey, April 30, 1923.

Chapter 15

1. Ruth Underhill, *The Navajos* (Norman: University of Oklahoma Press, 1967), 166.

2. Ibid., 168.

3. Ibid., 200–203.

4. *The Vanishing American,* 150.

5. Z.G. Letter to Dolly Grey, March 16, 1924. Grey also added that he thought of withdrawing the manuscript, but the movie and book were timed to debut together.

6. Z.G. Letter to William Briggs, May 23, 1924.

7. This was historical fact. The influenza epidemic spread throughout the world after the war.

8. *The Vanishing American,* 301. Grey the moral critic surfaces here.

9. See the reprint edition of *The Vanishing American* (1982) for the original version.

Chapter 16

1. Grey wrote a total of 89 books, 56 of which were western novels, plus four collections of novelettes and short stories. For a complete list of novels, short stories, articles, and films see Gruber, Farley, or Scott.

2. Gruber, 187.

3. Kant, 40.

4. For a complete account of Grey's break with Arizona see G. M. Farley's "Zane Grey's Fight with Arizona," *The Zane Grey Collector,* May 4, 1971.

5. See Carlos Baker's *Hemingway* (New York: Charles Scribner's Sons, 1969), 271. This is indicative of Hemingway's skewed thinking. He probably, in truth, envied Grey's fishing skills. When Grey's *Tales of Fishes* appeared in 1919, the young Hemingway was one of its adoring fans.

6. Gruber, 224.

7. Ibid.

8. Kant, 151.

9. Gruber, 253.

Chapter 17

1. Cited in Gruber, 164.

Selected References

The Novels of Zane Grey

Listed below are the significant novels of Zane Grey that I have mentioned or discussed in detail in this book; also listed are the books that I have consulted frequently during the preparation. They cover the years 1903 (his first novel) through Grey's death in 1939, the period analyzed in *Zane Grey: Romancing the West*. I have departed from traditional bibliographical format to give the reader a year-by-year list of accomplishments. For each novel I have listed title, date of publication, and publisher. Readers seeking a complete primary source bibliography should consult Carlton Jackson's *Zane Grey* or Kenneth William Scott's *Zane Grey: Born to the West*.

1903
Betty Zane   Charles Francis Press

1906
The Spirit of the Border   A. L. Burt and Company

1908
The Last of the Plainsmen   Outing Publishing Company

1909

The Last Trail   Outing Publishing Company

The Short Stop   A. C. McClurg and Company

1910

The Heritage of the Desert   Harper and Brothers

The Young Forester   Harper and Brothers

1911

The Young Pitcher   Harper and Brothers

1912

Riders of the Purple Sage   Harper and Brothers

Ken Ward in the Jungle   Harper and Brothers

1913

Desert Gold   Harper and Brothers

1914

The Light of Western Stars   Harper and Brothers

1915

The Lone Star Ranger   Harper and Brothers

The Rainbow Trail   Harper and Brothers

1916

The Border Legion   Harper and Brothers

1917

Wildfire   Harper and Brothers

1918

The U.P. Trail   Harper and Brothers

1919

The Desert of Wheat   Harper and Brothers

1920

Man of the Forest   Harper and Brothers

1921

The Mysterious Rider   Harper and Brothers

1922

To the Last Man   Harper and Brothers
The Day of the Beast   Harper and Brothers

1923

Wanderer of the Wasteland   Harper and Brothers
Tappan's Burro and Other Stories
   (novelette and short stories)   Harper and Brothers

1924

Call of the Canyon   Harper and Brothers

1925

The Thundering Herd   Harper and Brothers
The Vanishing American   Harper and Brothers

1926

Under the Tonto Rim   Harper and Brothers

1927

Forlorn River   Harper and Brothers

1928

Nevada   Harper and Brothers
Wild Horse Mesa   Harper and Brothers

1929

Fighting Caravans   Harper and Brothers

1930

The Wolf Tracker   Harper and Brothers
The Shepherd of Guadaloupe   Harper and Brothers

1931

Sunset Pass	Harper and Brothers

1932

Arizona Ames	Harper and Brothers
Robber's Roost	Harper and Brothers

1933

The Drift Fence	Harper and Brothers
The Hash Knife Outfit	Harper and Brothers

1934

Code of the West	Harper and Brothers

1935

Thunder Mountain	Harper and Brothers

1936

The Trail Driver	Harper and Brothers
The Lost Wagon Train	Harper and Brothers

1937

West of the Pecos	Harper and Brothers

1938

Raiders of Spanish Peaks	Harper and Brothers

1939

Knights of the Range	Harper and Brothers
Western Union	Harper and Brothers

Articles by Zane Grey

"Arizona Bear." *Country Gentleman*, 11 December 1920.
"Arizona Bear." *Country Gentleman*, 18 December 1920.
"Bear Trails." *Country Gentleman*, 3 March 1923.
"Bear Trails." *Country Gentleman*, 10 March 1923.
"Bear Trails." *Country Gentleman*, 17 March 1923.

"Colorado Trails." In *Zane Grey: Outdoorsman.* Edited by George Reiger. Englewood Cliffs, N.J.: Prentice-Hall, 1972.

"Death Valley." *Harpers,* May 1920.

"Down Into the Desert." *Ladies Home Journal,* January 1924.

"Keys to Greatness." *Coronet,* May 1951.

"My Own Life." In *Zane Grey: The Man and His Work.* New York: Harper and Brothers, 1928.

"Nonnezoshe, the Rainbow Bridge." In *Zane Grey Outdoorsman.* Edited by George Reiger. Englewood Cliffs, N.J.: Prentice Hall, 1972.

"The Living Past." *Zane Grey Collector* 7, no. 2 (1972).

"The Man Who Influenced Me Most." *American Magazine,* August 1926.

"Tonto Basin." In *Zane Grey: Outdoorsman.* Edited by George Reiger. Englewood Cliffs, N.J.: Prentice Hall, 1972.

"Tonto Bear." *Country Gentleman,* 8 March 1924.

"What the Desert Means to Me." *American Magazine,* November 1924.

"What the Open Means to Me." In *Zane Grey: The Man and His Work.* New York: Harper and Brothers, 1928.

Unpublished Material

Beard, Daniel. Daniel Beard Papers: Library of Congress, Washington, D.C.

Davis, Robert Hobart. Robert Hobart Davis Papers. New York Public Library, New York City, New York.

Deland, Margaret. Margaret Deland Collection. Colby College, Waterville, Maine.

Farley, G. M. G. M. Farley Collection. Hagerstown, Maryland.

Garland, Hamlin. Hamlin Garland Collection. University of Southern California, Los Angeles, California.

Grey, Zane. Zane Grey Collection. Beinecke Rare Book and Manuscript Library, Yale University Library, New Haven, Connecticut.

———. Zane Grey Collection. Clifton Waller Barrett Library, University of Virginia, Charlottesville, Virginia.

———. Zane Grey Collection. The Elmer Holmes Bobst Library, New York University, New York City, New York.

———. Zane Grey Collection. The Harry Ransom Humanities Research Center, University of Texas at Austin, Austin, Texas.

———. Zane Grey Collection. Houghton Library, Harvard University, Cambridge, Massachusetts.

————. Zane Grey Collection. Los Angeles Public Library, Los Angeles, California.

————. Zane Grey Collection. Pierpont Morgan Library, New York City, New York.

————. Zane Grey Collection. Zane Grey Home, Lackawaxen, Pennsylvania.

————. Zane Grey Incorporated, Woodland Hills, California.

Hitchcock, Ripley. Ripley Hitchcock Collection. Rare Book and Manuscript Library, Columbia University Library, New York City, New York.

Jansen, Roy. Roy Jansen Collection. State Library of Pennsylvania, Harrisburg, Pennsylvania.

Markham, Edwin. Edwin Markham Collection. Horrman Library, Wagner College, New York City, New York.

Page, Thomas Nelson. Thomas Nelson Page Papers. William R. Perkins Library, Duke University Library, Durham, North Carolina.

Parsons, George W. George W. Parsons Collection. Arizona Historical Society, Tucson, Arizona.

Rust, David Dexter. David Dexter Rust Papers. Church of Jesus Christ of Latter-Day Saints, Historical Department, Salt Lake City, Utah.

Secondary Sources

BOOKS

Berkhofer, Robert F., Jr. *The White Man's Indian: Images of the American Indian from Columbus to the Present.* New York: Random House, 1978.

Bolton, Herbert E. *Coronado: Knight of Pueblos and Plains.* Albuquerque: University of New Mexico Press, 1949.

Branch, Douglas. *The Cowboy and His Interpreters.* New York: Cooper Square Publishers, 1961.

Calder, Jennie. *There Must be a Lone Ranger: The American West in Film and Reality.* London: Hamish Hamilton, 1974.

Cawelti, John. *Adventure, Mystery, and Romance: Formula Stories as Art and Popular Culture.* Chicago: University of Chicago Press, 1976.

————. *The Six-Gun Mystique.* Bowling Green, Ohio: Bowling Green University Popular Press, 1971.

Churchill, Allen. *The Literary Decade.* Englewood Cliffs, N.J.: Prentice-Hall, 1971.

Cumberland, Charles C. *Mexican Revolution: The Constitutional Years.* Austin: University of Texas Press, 1972.

Dobie, J. Frank. *Guide to Life and Literature of the Southwest.* Dallas, Texas: Southern Methodist University Press, 1952.

Dutton, Bertha P. *American Indians of the Southwest.* Albuquerque: University of New Mexico Press, 1983.

Easton, Robert. *Max Brand, The Big Westerner.* Norman: University of Oklahoma Press, 1970.

Easton, Robert, and Mackenzie Brown. *Lord of Beasts: The Life of Buffalo Jones.* Tucson: University of Arizona Press, 1961.

Erisman, Fred, and Richard W. Etulain, eds. *Fifty Western Writers: A Bio-Bibliographical Guide.* Westport, Conn.: Greenwood Press, 1982.

Everson, William K. *A Pictorial History of the Western Film.* Secaucus, N.J.: The Citadel Press, 1969.

Faust, Friedrich Schiller. *Notebooks and Poems* (unpublished).

Fenin, George N., and William K. Everson. *The Western: From Silents to Cinerama.* New York: Orion Press, 1962.

Frantz, Joe B., and Julian Ernest Choate, Jr. *The American Cowboy: The Myth and the Reality.* Norman: University of Oklahoma Press, 1955.

Gay, Carol. *Zane Grey, Story Teller.* Columbus, Ohio: State Library of Ohio, 1979.

Gruber, Frank. *Zane Grey: A Biography.* New York: Signet, 1971.

Hutchinson, W. H. *The World, the Work, and the West of W. H. D. Koerner.* Norman: University of Oklahoma Press, 1978.

Jackson, Carlton. *Zane Grey.* Rev. ed. Twayne's United States Authors Series. Boston: G. K. Hall and Company, 1989.

Kant, Candace C. *Zane Grey's Arizona.* Flagstaff: Northland Publishing, 1984.

Kerr, Jean. *Zane Grey, Man of the West.* New York: Grosset and Dunlap, 1949.

Kimball, Arthur G. *Ace of Hearts: The Westerns of Zane Grey.* Fort Worth: Texas Christian University Press, 1993.

Lasky, Jesse L., with Don Weldon. *I Blow My Own Horn.* Garden City, N.Y.: Doubleday, 1957.

Leish, Kenneth W. *Cinema.* New York: Newsweek Books, 1974.

Lyon, Thomas, ed. *A Literary History of the American West.* Fort Worth: Texas Christian University Press, 1987.

McNitt, Frank. *The Indian Traders.* Norman: University of Oklahoma Press, 1962.

McWilliams, Carey. *North From Mexico: The Spanish-Speaking People of the United States.* New York: Greenwood Press, 1968.

Nachbar, Jack, ed. *Focus on the Western.* Englewood Cliffs, N.J.: Prentice-Hall, 1974.

Nash, Roderick. *The Nervous Generation: American Thought, 1917–1930.* Chicago: Rand McNally, 1970.

Nicholas, John H. *Tom Mix: Riding up to Glory.* Kansas City, Missouri: The Lowell Press, A Persimmon Hill Book, 1980.

Nye, Russel B. *The Unembarrassed Muse: The Popular Arts in America.* New York: Dial Press, 1979.

Parkes, Henry Bamford. *A History of Mexico.* Boston: Houghton Mifflin Company, 1969.

Reiger, George, ed. *Zane Grey: Outdoorsman.* Englewood Cliffs, N.J.: Prentice-Hall, 1972.

Ronald, Ann. *Zane Grey.* Boise, Idaho: Boise State University Press, 1975.

Rusho, W. L. and Gregory C. Crampton. *Desert River Crossing: Historic Lee's Ferry on the Colorado River.* Santa Barbara, California: Peregrine-Smith, 1981.

Schatz, Thomas. *Hollywood Genres: Formulas, Filmmaking and the Studio System.* Philadelphia: Temple University Press, 1981.

Schneider, Norris F. *Zane Grey: The Man Whose Books Made the West Famous.* Zanesville, Ohio: Norris F. Schneider, 1967.

Scott, Kenneth William. *Zane Grey: Born to the West.* Boston: G. K. Hall, 1979.

Selden, Rodman. *A Short History of Mexico.* New York: Stein and Day, Publishers, 1982.

Smith, Henry Nash. *Virgin Land: The American West as Symbol and Myth.* New York: Vintage Books, 1957.

Sonnichsen, C. L. *From Hopalong to Hud: Thoughts on Western Fiction.* College Station, Texas: Texas A&M University Press, 1978.

Stevenson, Robert Louis. *The Amateur Emigrant.* London: The Hogarth Press, 1984.

Tuska, Jon. *The Filming of the West.* Garden City, N.Y.: Doubleday, 1976.

Underhill, Ruth. *The Navajos.* Norman: University of Oklahoma Press, 1967.

Womack, John Jr. *Zapata and the Mexican Revolution.* New York: Alfred A. Knopf, 1971.

Woody, Clara T., and Milton J. Schwartz. *Globe, Arizona: Early Times in a Little World of Copper and Cattle.* Tucson: Arizona Historical Society, 1977.

Zane Grey: The Man and His Work. New York: Harper and Brothers, 1928.

Arrington, Leonard, and Jon Haupt. "Community and Isolation: Some Aspects of Mormon Westerns." *Western American Literature,* vol. 8 (1973).

Boyle, R. H. "The Man Who Lived Two Lives in One." *Sports Illustrated,* 29 April 1968.

Cawelti, John. "God's Country, Las Vegas, and the Gun Fighter: Differing Visions of the West." *Western American Literature,* vol. 9 (February 1975).

———. "The Gunfighter and Society." *American West,* vol. 5 (March 1968).

———. "Savagery, Civilization and the Western Hero." In *Focus on the Western,* edited by Jack Nachbar. Englewood Cliffs, N.J.: Prentice-Hall, 1974.

Dedera, D. "Shame of the Rim Now Its Showcase." *Arizona Days and Ways,* 29 March 1964.

Early, Elinor. "He Made the West Famous." *True West,* March 1969.

Elkin, Frederick. "The Psychological Appeal for Children of the Hollywood B Western." In *Focus on the Western,* edited by Jack Nachbar. Englewood Cliffs, N.J.: Prentice-Hall, 1974.

Etulain, Richard W. "Cultural Origins of the Western." In *Focus on the Western,* edited by Jack Nachbar. Englewood Cliffs, N.J.: Prentice-Hall, 1974.

———. "A Dedication to the Memory of Zane Grey." *Arizona and the West,* vol. 12 (Autumn 1970).

Farley, G. M. "Zane Grey and the Great Outdoors." *Zane Grey Western,* vol. 5 (1973).

———. "Zane Grey, Man of the West." *Real West,* September 1972.

———. "Zane Grey's Arizona." *Zane Grey Collector,* vol. 4 (1971).

———. "Zane Grey's Fight with Arizona." *Zane Grey Collector,* vol. 4 (1971).

Folsom, James K. "Westerns as Social and Political Alternatives." In *Focus on the Western,* edited by Jack Nachbar. Englewood Cliffs, N.J.: Prentice-Hall, 1974.

Goble, Danny. "The Days That Were No More: A Look at Zane Grey's West." *Journal of Arizona History,* vol. 14 (Spring 1973).

"Goettle's Zane Grey's Cabin." *Tonto Trails,* Summer 1981.

Hayden, Mike. "Fishing Zane Grey's River." *Field and Stream,* October 1962.

Helminiak, Raymond. "The About-Face of a Buffalo Hunter." *Frontier Times,* November 1971.

"Heroes Ride on Forever." *Time,* 19 June 1950.

Homans, Peter. "Puritanism Revisited: An Analysis of the Contemporary

Screen Image Western." In *Focus on the Western,* edited by Jack Nachbar. Englewood Cliffs, N.J.: Prentice-Hall, 1974.

Hough, Donald. "The Great Kaibab Deer Drive." *Zane Grey Collector,* vol. 4 (1971).

Kimball, Arthur G. "My Navajo Oasis: Irony in Grey's *Heritage of the Desert.*" *South Dakota Review,* vol. 28 (Summer 1990).

Kimball, Ethel. "Trail to Thunder Mountain." *True West,* March 1973.

Kitses, Jim. "The Western Ideology and Archetype." In *Focus on the Western* edited by Jack Nachbar. Englewood Cliffs, N.J.: Prentice-Hall, 1974.

Mead, Norman W. "Zane Grey, the Man Whose Books Made the West Famous Lived Here." *Arizona Highways,* October 1973.

Moses, Montrose J. "Zane Grey, Literary Craftsman." *The Book News Monthly,* February 1918.

Netherby, Steve. "Zane Grey: Author, Angler, and Explorer." *Field and Stream,* January 1972.

"New York's Awe at the Best Seller." *The Literary Digest,* 10 March 1923.

"Obituary." *Newsweek,* 30 October 1939.

Olsen, T. V. "Zane Grey: How He Grew." *The Roundup,* September 1966.

———. "Zane Grey: The Writer and His West." *The Roundup,* October 1966.

Peeples, Samuel A. "Zane Grey: The Man Who Influenced Me Most." *Zane Grey Collector,* vol. 4 (1971).

"Return of Zane Grey." *Newsweek,* 12 September 1955.

Roberts, Gary L. "The West's Gunmen, Part I." *American West,* vol. 8 (January 1971).

———. "The West's Gunmen, Part II." *American West,* vol. 8 (March 1971).

Stanley, R. "Legacy from Lo-Lomai." *Westways,* May 1956.

Stocker, Joseph. "Zane Grey and Pleasant Valley." *Westways,* February 1960.

Tallon, James. "Zane Grey's Rim: Coconino and Sitegreaves National Forests, Arizona." *Travel,* June 1975.

Topping, Gary. "Zane Grey's West." *Journal of Popular Culture,* vol. 7 (Winter 1973).

Tuska, Jon. "The American Western Cinema: 1903–Present." In *Focus on the Western,* edited by Jack Nachbar. Englewood Cliffs, N.J.: Prentice-Hall, 1974.

Woody, Clara T., and Milton L. Schwartz. "War in Pleasant Valley: The Outbreak of The Graham-Tewksbury Feud." *The Journal of Arizona History,* vol. 18 (1977).

Index

A Note about the Author

A literary historian, essayist, and novelist, Stephen J. May is on the faculty of Colorado Northwestern College in Craig, Colorado. His other books include *Pilgrimage, Footloose on the Santa Fe Trail,* and *Fire from the Skies.* He is a former contributing editor of *Southwest Art* and is a member of the Colorado Authors' League.